S0-AUP-228

with best wishes

Rudy y.

On the cover

Diego Maradona (left) dazzles the crowd and his
opponents with his dribbling skills at the 1990
World Cup in Italy.

Allsport Photo.

The author would like to thank all the players and coaches who inspired and helped create this book. In my thirty years of soccer, I have played with and coached some great players and people. This book is dedicated to all of them.

SOCCER FOR EVERYONE

Rudy Yakzan

© First Edition, 1999
Oceanprises Publications
1548 San Alto, Orange, CA 92865
ISBN 0-9676720-0-7

www.Soccer-HQ.com

Table of Contents

Forward

Soccer is the world's greatest sport. It is exhilarating to play, exciting to watch, and fun to learn. It's not a coincidence that soccer dominates all sports in almost every country around the world, and the World Cup is the grandest sporting event on earth, bigger even than the Olympics. Soccer is an aerobic sport that requires and improves coordination, skill, strength, endurance, and speed. It also improves perseverance, character, cooperation, brains, and emotion. Learning the game means learning and refining all of the above qualities, as well as improving soccer skills. This book will teach *anyone* interested in the game how to think and play the best soccer possible.

Considering the pool talent and resources in this country, soccer should become a successful and popular sport. Yet, soccer has not quite moved up from the back seat of American sports and feeble media coverage. Changing attitudes after the Women's World Cup and other major events will help change public interest. Perhaps the most important attitude of all is the public's perception of the game as a popular one or not. We believe this should start at a recreational level where *anyone* who wants to play can go out and play at the local park, school, or any patch of dirt or grass…that's how the rest of the world does it, why can't we?

If we were to wait for the media to pick up soccer as a national sport, we would have to wait forever. People who enjoy the game will have to go out and play, practice and improve. This book will help you do just that. The premise of this book is simplifying the information that describes the game, rather than use complicated "coach talk." Readers who understand English can understand the simple concepts within this book, whether they have some soccer experience or none. Therefore, we can rightly say that this book *is* for everyone.

Win or lose the game...it seems that everyone wins when playing soccer.

Forward

Chapter I

The Fundamentals

- *Passing*

- *Trapping*

- *Kicking*

- *Dribbling*

- *Tackling*

- *Heading*

Soccer is an easy game to play, and learning the basic fundamentals is both simple and fun. It is not unusual to have athletic or coordinated individuals who learn the game as late as their teens or twenties and show good passing or dribbling skills. This is perhaps why there is an untapped recreational soccer pool talent in this country. Many athletic individuals have shown that learning basic soccer fundamentals can be easy and quick. Kicking, dribbling, trapping, and heading the ball are the fundamental skills that constitute the majority of soccer action, and they can *all* be learned easily.

Passing

*P*assing is probably the most fundamental soccer skill. Since soccer is a team sport, the ball is passed more times than it is kicked, headed, trapped, or thrown. As in any other skill, the best method to learn and improve is through application and repetition. There are many passing drills that help improve a player's passing ability and accuracy. They all naturally encompass repetitive passing to moving or stationary targets.

The best way to pass the ball is by using the inside of the foot (some call it the inseam) for maximum control and accuracy. While it is possible to pass using various styles and parts of the foot, the most fundamental passing technique has always encompassed using the inside of the foot to contact the ball.

A top view showing how the foot contacts the ball in a typical pass.

The Fundamentals

The photos in this section show some drills that keep the players' attention, as well as improve their passing. These drills include a variety of scenarios, such as passing to stationary targets/teammates, passing to moving targets, passing between targets, short passes, long passes, etc. They also include a variety of sub-skills such as kicking with either side of the foot, or using the heel or top of the foot to deliver a pass.

Advanced passing skills may include passing with either foot, passing while dribbling the ball, passing to open space, and passing "patterns," or what many players refer to as "squares" and "triangles." Regardless of their skill levels, players can improve their passing game by continuous practice and consistency. Coaches can pinpoint the strength and weaknesses of individual players and have them improve in certain areas. Beginners, for example, tend to need work in positioning their body and feet for a good kick, while many experienced players with good foot skills may need improvement in their "passing vision," or the ability to mentally spot or diagram a good pass.

Passing drills should be an easy welcome to the sport, and not too complicated, especially for beginners. As mentioned earlier, this is an easy game to grasp, and passing is the most fundamental of skills. It is best for coaches to let players improve and grow at their own pace rather than over-coach them on how to pass a soccer ball. Accuracy and consistency will eventually follow if the player is interested and determined.

Trapping/receiving

*W*hen a ball is passed to a player, he or she needs to receive and control it. Trapping is the most common method of receiving and keeping possession of the ball. The most common trap requires using the inside of the foot to cushion the ball as it arrives. Players can also

The player watches the ball and controls it as it makes contact with his foot. The toe is pointed slightly upwards on the trapping foot.

The chest trap is commonly used to collect aerial balls.

use other parts of their feet or bodies, such as the outside of the foot, the chest, thigh, or belly to cushion and trap a ball. Hands and arms are of course off limits and some other areas such as knees and shins are not good for trapping the ball since it can easily bounce off of these bony areas.

Since the inside of the foot does most of the trapping, players can raise their feet or use their bodies to meet an incoming ball at any height. When doing so, it is common for a player to point the inside of the foot downward to bring the ball down after it contacts the inseam. Although these are good general guidelines, some players can trap the ball using

Her eyes upon the ball, a player raises her foot to meet and collect an aerial pass.

unconventional methods, such as blocking it with both legs, or using their cleats to receive the ball. While these methods may work, they have a higher margin of error than conventional trapping with the inside of the foot.

Players can practice trapping and passing at the same time. Each pass requires a trap of some sort, and players can work in pairs on both skills simultaneously. One of the sub-skills associated with trapping the ball requires quick movement to get to the ball. Not all passes are perfect or designed to reach a teammate's feet. Therefore, quick feet and running to meet he ball are important sub-skills for effective trapping. One must get to the ball to be able to receive it.

Although trapping is a fundamental skill, it will probably take more practice and time to master. One can truly appreciate the excellent receiving skills of professional players who trap the ball so easily and effortlessly. These players did not reach this level overnight, and they undoubtedly perfected it through proper application and training. One of the most glaring differences between beginners and advanced players is their trapping ability. Watching an amateur game, one can notice several missed and unsuccessful traps, which is quite rare on an international or professional level. Coaches should emphasize the importance of trapping to their players, and teach them the proper techniques for this skill.

The Fundamentals

Kicking

*T*here are many differences between *kicking* and passing the ball. The primary differences lay in intent and velocity. A pass is meant to transfer possession of the ball from one teammate to another, and it is usually delivered with measured force so the teammate can receive and control it. Players usually kick a ball with much more force to score on a goalie, cross it across the field, or to clear it from one's defensive area. To generate the most power, players use the top of the foot to contact the ball, otherwise known as "kicking from the laces." To do so, a player bends the knee and snaps the lower leg delivering the most amount of power. American football field goal kickers have almost all switched to soccer-style kicking to gain the most distance and accuracy. Players can also kick the ball with the inside of the foot for added accuracy, but this sacrifices power considerably.

Anatomy of a kick: the left foot is planted next to the ball; the right leg bent backwards and ready to strike.

One of the keys to kicking is planting the opposite foot next to the ball. What this means is placing the left foot near the ball if kicking with the right, and vice versa. The actual distance from the planting foot to the ball may vary with the player's technique, and the way that he or she wants to kick the ball. Consistency in placing the foot, however, is important and one can attain this through practice. Coaches can demonstrate kicking techniques to their players by showing them first the importance of planting the opposite foot. They can also explain how varying the distance of the planting foot from the ball can change the trajectory of the ball.

By kicking the ball from beneath, or making contact close to the ground, a player can loft the ball or give it a high trajectory of travel. When kicked near the top, the ball tends to skip on the grass. Good players and strikers in particular can vary their kicks to beat goalies low or high using different kicking techniques. Consequently, when crossing the ball, it is always contacted low so it can rise, and when kicked against a good goalie, it is best to try and beat him low. Advanced players can kick the ball from one side or the other (as opposed to dead center) to "bend" it or give it an unpredictable trajectory. This means the ball can follow a

This is what a kick looks like from the planting foot side. Note the proximity of the left foot to the ball.

banana-like trajectory in reaching its final destination. This "banana" kick is quite popular on free kicks to avoid defensive walls and confuse a goalkeeper's judgment. Another advanced technique includes chipping the ball, which may work well against a goalie that comes up too far off his line.

This view shows the angled approach a player usually takes while kicking a ball.

Practicing kicks is the best exercise to improve technique. Players can do this individually against a wall or in groups shooting at a goal or at each other. Kicking a stationary ball is much easier than a moving one, so it's a good idea to practice dribbling and shooting on the run as well. This drill has many variants to it that include cutting left and right before taking the shot. Since most goals are scored from good kicks, coaches should put their players –especially forwards and midfielders- through various kicking drills every practice.

This close-up shows how the kicker's foot makes contact with the ball(kicking from the laces).

To kick the ball high, the foot makes low contact with the ball and "lifts" it high.

Dribbling

*D*ribbling a soccer ball requires more skill and coordination than passing or kicking. Dribbling requires many sub-skills that players can acquire with practice, or in the case of a few gifted athletes, come naturally and effortlessly. Dribbling skills include the ability to "protect" the ball with the body, and tapping the ball with the right amount of energy to keep it moving, but not too far out of reach. As players master these subtle but essential skills, they can increase their dribbling speed while controlling the ball.

Good dribblers can use either foot to control and tap the ball, as well as using either side of the foot. They can also switch their body positioning around the rolling ball to keep it away from pursuing and waiting defenders. Speed, acceleration, and body control are essential to good dribbling. Some players have been described as having the ball on a shoelace while gliding effortlessly with a ball at their feet.

Dribbling with control requires quick feet and constantly changing the pace.

Dribbling effectively in open space should be a simple task to any good soccer player. The keys here are to stay close to the ball and be able to tap the ball and vary the speed accordingly. Dribbling to beat players requires a little more skill, such as feinting to one side and going the other, as well as using quick acceleration to go past the defender. Another form of dribbling involves shielding the ball from an opponent and being able to turn with it or pass it off to a teammate. We will discuss some of these advanced dribbling techniques later in this book.

One of the most popular dribbling skills is the cone slalom. Others include dribbling in straight lines and releasing the ball to a teammate headed in the opposite direction who in turn repeats the same skill.

Tackling

*S*occer is a game with frequent changes of possession. The most direct method of dispossessing opponents is through various types of tackles. Ideally, a player should commit to tackle when he or she knows there is defensive support in case of a miss, or in case there is no doubt of a successful tackle, and sometimes when it's absolutely essential to dispossess a player in a scoring position.

There are three kinds of tackles commonly used by soccer players in all parts of the field. The first is the *poke tackle*, which somehow resembles its name. A player usually tries a poke tackle when the opponent brings the ball to approximately one step away from the defender. The defender can reach with his foot and "poke" the ball

The poke tackle: the defender (right) lunges forward and pokes the ball at the right moment.

away from the attacker, whether the two are facing each other, or running in the same direction.

The second type of tackle is the *block tackle*, which again resembles its description. In this case, the defender can block the ball with his foot and kick it cleanly, whether the dribbler tries to resist with a counter block or not. The keys to blocking the ball include locking the ankle for added strength (by raising the foot upward), and making contact with the instep.

The block tackle: the defender blocks the ball by locking his ankle and pointing the toes upward. This gives him better leverage than the attacker, whose foot is pointed downward.

Finally, the third type of tackle is one of the most spectacular plays in soccer: the *slide tackle*. Contrary to the belief that the slide tackle is used solely to stop an attacker on a breakaway, the slide tackle may be used on any part of the field to dispossess an opponent. The primary reason for attempting a slide tackle is *reach*. By extending the body and leading with the feet first, the defender can reach the ball, which may be partially blocked by the attacker. This tackle is especially effective in wet conditions that allow the defender to slide more toward target.

The Fundamentals

Whenever making a slide tackle, the defender must make contact with the ball first. If he contacts the player before the ball, the referee may not only whistle a foul, but may show a yellow or even a red card, depending on the angle, severity and circumstances involving the foul (attempt to injure, or deliberately fouling from behind). Players attempting the slide tackle must remember that by going down, they eliminate themselves from the play until they can stand again. Therefore, they should use good judgment when to leave their feet for a slide tackle.

The slide tackle: the defender slides his body and gets to the ball. He is in position to kick the ball or control it. The attacker can only jump to avoid tripping over the legal tackle.

For example, it's perfectly all right to attempt a slide tackle in the opposition's half. A slide tackle that results in a red card in that zone, however, may be inexcusable. The risk of earning a warning or ejection for a simple possession does not meet the reward. A sweeper who chases down a forward streaking on goal, however, must try to put himself in a position to attempt a last-ditch sliding tackle.

Heading

Watching modern soccer, one can see the importance of the "aerial" game and heading skills. Some think that France's Zinedine Zidane single-handedly beat mighty Brazil in 1998 with two brilliant flash headers he scored off of routine corner kicks. Zidane isn't the only great player who knows how to use his head in a game, and headers today account for a great share of goals scored. Heading the ball is equally important to defend against such aerial attacks, or to obtain dominance in midfield.

Heading the ball comfortably is a very important soccer skill.

Heading is one of the weakest skills of young American players today. This is perhaps due to a lack of emphasis on heading in training or in games, or to misconceptions regarding the safety of heading a soccer ball.

With proper training and attitude, players can learn to

head the ball safely and effectively. The most important mechanic in heading entails using the *feet* to *get* to the ball. Players should understand that without quick movement, the chances of the ball making contact with their heads are quite low, regardless of the accuracy of the friendly pass or cross! Therefore, the first sub-skill associated with heading includes running quickly toward the floating ball. The second skill usually includes timing the jump to make contact with the ball since players rarely have the luxury of heading the ball without leaving their feet or getting challenged by opponents. Coaches can teach their players how these skills by simply tossing the ball a short distance in the air and having the players "attack" and head it. As the players' skills and confidence increase, the distance can increase to corner kick length or more.

The next point that coaches can teach their players is keeping the eyes on the ball the entire time while trying to contact the ball. The eyes will shut automatically when the ball makes contact, but unless players can see the ball, they cannot make clean contact with it. This is of course true of any sport where athletes must keep their eyes on the ball for the best results. By keeping their eyes on the ball, players can also contact it with the correct part of the head.

If a player wears an imaginary headband, the correct parts of the head used to contact the ball are the areas covered by that headband on the front and sides of the head. One reason young players shy away from heading the ball is that it really hurts if it lands on the top or back of the head. The upper part of the forehead is nicely designed and protected to head the ball accurately and strongly. Players will also head the ball with equal strength using the side of the head while snapping their whole upper body at the moment of contact.

The whole body can be used as a bow that launches the ball that contacts the head. One of the reasons for the high numbers scored by headers is that goalkeepers cannot usually guess how the ball will bounce or skip off a players' head. It is much easier for goalies to "read" a kick taken by a left or right footer, and to anticipate when the kicker will make contact with that ball. It is usually much harder to anticipate a header on goal, especially during the aerial melees that can take place in front of goal. This gives the header an added value in front of the goal, whether offensively or defensively.

Just as kicks can vary in their aims, so can headers. The head can be used to gently pass the ball to a teammate, to score goals, to clear the defensive zone, or even to juggle or receive the ball. Coaches should instill an understanding of how to head the ball in each area of the field, and how to dictate the nature of the game through "aerial supremacy."

Finally, a discussion of heading today would not be complete without a mention of some of the latest studies that show heading may cause some injury. It is obvious that making contact with other heads, the goal post and even the ball may be painful and injurious. Therefore, coaches and players should use common sense when practicing headers. It is interesting to note that these same studies showed that soccer had higher injury rates than swimming and running, but much less than football and basketball. Soccer players in general are some of the most intelligent and articulate athletes on and off the field, so apparently, heading the ball does not affect the vast majority of players. One should take necessary precautions, however, especially with young children (whatever precautions dictated by the leagues/teams or common sense).

The player leaps to meet the ball in the air.

Chapter II

Becoming a Soccer Player

- *Goalkeeping*

- *The Art of Defense*

- *Playing Outside Back*

- *Playing Central Defense*

- *Different Defensive Roles*

- *The Midfield Generals*

- *Playing Outside Midfield*

- *The Central Links*

- *The Snipers*

As we mentioned earlier, it is not unusual for young athletes and adults who have never played the game to learn and master the majority of its skills. This section describes the tangible and subtle qualities that make a soccer player, regardless of what position he or she plays.

The first attribute of soccer players is their physical shape. Unlike American football and baseball, where physical size and strength are quite important, soccer players must be in good physical shape, and not necessarily big and strong. Aerobic shape is important to keep players on the field for 90 minutes, but players with less than perfect shape can counterbalance this deficiency with good skills and experience. Players should maintain a practice regime that improves skills and physical endurance. Many coaches believe that playing soccer is the most effective method to get in shape, while practicing and drilling can improve individual skills. Weight lifting can strengthen a player's legs to withstand the harsh contact during a game, and running laps and sprints can improve speed and endurance.

Finally, players need the right attitude to enjoy and succeed in soccer. This attitude includes the ability to study the game, enjoy time on the field, and play whenever possible. In other words, if more Americans treated soccer with the same reverence given to other sports, it would be just as popular and successful as American football and baseball.

In order to play the game in an organized and efficient manner, players must also learn certain roles and skills that enhance team play and chemistry. This includes having a strong team spirit, but more importantly, a strong understanding of how to play a certain position. Although attitude is quite important, if players lack the skills and experience to play certain positions, even the most positive attitude cannot save the team from certain defeat. Therefore, this section describes the ideal characteristics of players and their positions on the field.

Goalkeeping

*G*oalkeepers are a special breed of soccer players. For one, they are the only players allowed to touch the ball with their hands. The majority of goalkeepers around the world resemble football linebackers in their physical appearance and size. Although not all goalies are tall, height can be a definite advantage, especially against crosses, or for stretching to make saves. Strength can also be advantageous in pushing off intruding forwards, or to cushion the tough collisions that can take place in front of goal.

Yet size, strength and physical presence are not enough to make a good goalkeeper. More important attributes include mental quickness, experience, leadership, and instinct. Good goalkeepers also possess intangible qualities that include pride, poise, and an ability to command their box. Experienced goalies are great communicators who constantly talk to their teammates and help marshal the defense in fluid and dead-ball situations. Even the most athletic goalkeepers are suspect if they cannot command the box and issue clear instructions against dangerous goal kicks. Goalies in this case must communicate their instructions to the defensive wall, using their voice and hands to ensure the best defense.

Raw players can be coached for the position if they have what it takes to become a goalie. Americans in general have very good eye-hand coordination, which helps when playing goalkeeper. One of the first things a goalie must learn is awareness of where he is in relation to his goalposts. This requires a little bit of practice and instinct, but a quick backward glance can help a beginning goalie gauge his position initially.

By coming out to cut the angle, the goalie gives the attacker much less room to shoot at.

As he gains experience, a good keeper can usually mark his position instinctively.

Positional play is key to goalkeeping. This is not much different than with hockey goaltenders that have to constantly cut the shooting angle to make saves. The key difference, however, is the much larger size of a soccer goal. Cutting the angle is a key ingredient to making saves, and coaches can train their goalies by showing them how to cut the angle depending on the shot's origin. To understand this, one should understand the concept of "near" and "far" post. Near post is the post closer to the shooter and therefore, the one easier to score on. Far post is the post behind the advanced goaltender, and farther from the shooter, therefore, it is harder to score on.

Goalkeepers need to always protect their near post since it is much easier to score on, which shifts the burden on the shooter to try and score on the far post. Additionally, most strikers traditionally go for the far post. Many goals are scored on the near post due to goalie error, or to the close proximity of the shooter to the goal, where defending it would have been very difficult. A goalie that allows a goal on the far post when positioned properly is not frowned upon as much as one who gets beat on the near post. Therefore, the first rule of positional goalkeeping: always defend the near post, and challenge the shooter to beat you on the more difficult far post.

Other than his brains and courage, a goalie's most important assets are his hands, which he can use for catching, punching and blocking the ball. Goalkeepers must usually make an instantaneous decision whether to catch a ball or deflect it away from danger. This of course depends on the velocity of the shot and the comfort level of the goaltender. To catch the

When punching high balls, the goalkeeper should punch them up and away at approximately a 45 - degree trajectory. Note the extended knee to help protect the otherwise exposed goalkeeper.

ball, the goalkeeper must use his arms and body to cradle it or prevent it from trickling through him. If he can't catch it, he should deflect it away from danger, preferably to a severe angle on the near side.

The goalie catches the ball and cradles it using his body for backup.

Goalkeeping coaches teach their players to deflect the ball at a 45-degree angle when punching it.

A goalie's hands (and brains) can help him avoid trouble before it ever happens. A good example is getting off the line and catching a good cross *before* it reaches an opponent. The goalkeeper is the only player on the field who can perform such a play. Even if he is the same size as all the players around him, he can reach higher by virtue of jumping and extending his arms. If he waits for shots to come his way, one or several will eventually score. Therefore, it's best to use good aggressive judgment and attack some balls before they end up on attackers' heads or feet. The hands may of course only be used inside the penalty box, and a goaltender can be ejected for handling a ball intentionally outside that area.

Becoming a Soccer Player

Goalkeepers must anticipate each play to give them a chance to make the saves. The position requires intense mental concentration, as well as physical strength and stamina. Some professional goalies have reported losing more than a few pounds in their body weight during games. This should not come as a big surprise considering the intensity of top-level games, especially when played in the heat, or in other trying conditions.

Competent goalies can watch plays develop before they enter their defensive zones. They must make quick decisions and adjustments to ensure they will be in a position to smother a play before it develops, or make saves if necessary. Since the new rules do not allow goalies to handle the ball if it's passed back by a teammate, goalkeepers must also have sufficient foot skills to control or get rid of the ball before an aggressive forward can steal it. This is an area of concern for many goalkeepers who may not be a match for the fleet-footed and opportunistic forwards.

If in doubt, the goalkeeper must always clear the ball quickly and aggressively rather than giving a fast forward the chance to steal it.

Another skill that goalies must possess is the ability to dive and stop low or middle balls. When diving, the goalkeeper should dive

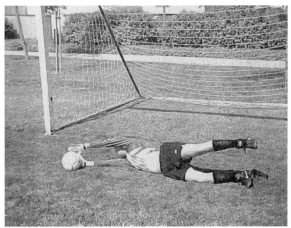

Analyzing a good dive: the goalie dives on his side; full extionsion for reach; the lower hand is behind the ball; the top hand on the ball to control it.

to his side, not on the stomach. This allows him to see the ball and use his hands and arms, as well as preventing injury to his ribs and vital organs. When diving, the lower arm must be fully extended for maximum reach and to prevent injury to elbows. The ball should be ideally tipped with the lower hand. When diving and catching the ball, the lower hand should block the ball and the upper one should be on top for maximum efficiency.

It is not a coincidence to have many goalkeepers as team captains. This is because the position entails having many leadership qualities. From their position, goalkeepers can view the entire field and watch the progress of the game without being overly involved in every play. This allows them to analyze the match objectively and therefore, ask their teammates to make adjustments. No position can influence the pace of the game than that of the goalkeeper. He can punt the ball quickly across the field, or dribble it lazily to waste time and frustrate opponents. He can also make inspirational saves that keep his team in the game, or allow soft goals that demoralize his teammates.

Goalkeepers shout more instructions in a match than anyone else, especially when setting up a defensive wall. Whatever their cultural norm, they must always keep in mind that most players are more inspired, rather than intimidated into action. Therefore, they must always deliver these instructions clearly, but use an acceptable tone and language that won't offend the same players who help defend their goals. Many young keepers watch their idols on television yell instructions and gesture wildly to their teammates as if they were angry or anxious. The reality is that these goalies usually play in full noisy stadiums that require them to yell and gesture wildly to be heard. This practice is usually unnecessary at amateur levels, and goalkeepers are better sticking to positive reinforcement rather than wild gestures and shouts.

Finally, this position has different rules that govern it than those that apply to field players. Some of these have recently changed, and may be subject to future change, therefore, we suggest you refer to recent copies of rulebooks that may govern your particular league or club. Different leagues may have different rules. FIFA rules, however are considered the norm (FIFA is soccer's international governing body). These rules basically prevent the goalkeeper from handling the ball outside the penalty box, or from touching the ball if it is *deliberately* passed from a teammate's foot. If the ball is deflected or passed using any legal part of the body (such as the head or chest), then the goalie may pick it up.

Once the ball is picked up, the goalkeeper may punt it or throw it. He may bounce it several times, and take a few steps before punting it. Also, although goalkeepers are masters of using the clock, their time-wasting tactics are subject to the referee's discretion, and they may be warned or cautioned with a yellow card for what the referee may consider as excessive time-wasting behavior. If a goalkeeper drops the ball and dribbles it, he or she cannot subsequently pick it up again to punt it, and most get rid of it by kicking it while it's on the ground.

One of the best ways to learn the intangible aspects of the position is to watch professional games and goalies. By analyzing their style and tactics, young goalkeepers can learn and adopt a style of their own. Some of the world's best goalkeepers today include Peter Shmeichel of Denmark and Manchester United fame (He recently transferred to Sporting Lisbon in Portugal). Schmeichel is a large and imposing figure in goal with his two-meter frame and fiery personality. Mexican Jorge Campos on the other hand is a small and quick goalie with cat-like reflexes and icy nerves. These two players represent two distinctly different and successful styles of goalkeeping.

The Art of Defense

*A*lthough a few pundits will disagree, most professional coaches believe that a team cannot succeed at high levels without an excellent defense. Many world-class coaches have blamed the lack of success with various teams due to a porous defense. The adjectives describing a poor defense outnumber any others in soccer: "The defense leaked, was unreliable, incompetent, unorganized." This author agrees that for a team to succeed, it must build upon a sound defensive unit centered upon reliable and smart defenders. As in every team sport, scorers still get most of the glory, and nothing excites a crowd as much as spectacular goals and counter goals. In the old adage of soccer lingo, however, defense wins or preserves wins.

To the chagrin of goal admirers, some of the world's most competent and perfect players are defenders. This is not unusual since coaches at amateur levels start by building teams with defenses made of the most reliable players. It is very hard to play catch-up in soccer, and much easier to defend a lead. Therefore, it makes sense to build a team from the back up. While some coaches and most crowds do not adhere to this philosophy, the relative low scoring in today's professional soccer indicates this trend.

The modern game is played with three to four defenders. While their alignment or assignments may differ, all must play competent individual and team defense. Traditionally, there are two types of defenders: outside and central ones.

Outside backs play on the flanks and employ their quickness and agility in chasing down and stopping outside attacks. In most professional teams, these backs are getting more and more involved in the attack to help their midfielders and forwards. Central defenders, on the other hand, must employ toughness in the middle, as well as use their good judgement in playing the offside rule or making timely tackles that won't jeopardize their position. In either case, most defenders know that they cannot afford to lose a tackle too many or lose position to an attacker. Therefore, they have to rely upon sound judgement, helpful teammates, and a good measure of physical fitness and strength. Lady luck is a not a friend of defenders, and the less they rely upon her, the better.

Playing outside back

*P*laying outside back requires its own tactics by virtue of the position. Many attacks start on the outside and develop down the wings before the ball is dribbled or passed inside. The primary duty of outside backs is to prevent these attacks from happening, or more realistically, from maturing into dangerous plays. Time is the defender's friend in this case, and the more he can cover and delay the attack from developing, the better. Patience is a defensive virtue, and good backs will not make poorly calculated or rash tackles that may or may not succeed, especially on the outside. By being patient and keeping the inside track, backs can get help from teammates, or pounce on the ball at the appropriate time.

Understanding the "inside line" is a necessary asset in playing defense. This simply means keeping position between the attacker and the goal. This requires facing the defender and backing up using quick movement. Many refer to this as "cat and mouse." The defender can be the cat, and the mouse is dribbling the ball and wants through. All the cat has to do is simply not let it through. The mouse tries really hard, but cannot get through since the cat is quick and uses very little energy to protect this imaginary inside line. A great exercise for defenders is to play this cat and mouse game without trying to get the ball, but simply moving laterally and backwards to block the path of the ball. By doing so patiently, they'll find that in 8 out of 10 times, most attackers will cough up the ball or dribble it too far on their own without defensive pressure. The real pressure is on the dribbler to go around a competent and agile defender.

It sounds easy, but most attackers aren't mice and some of the best dribblers in the game roam free on the wings. Therefore, timing comes into play, and defenders must know when and how to get the ball and how get help from teammates. To play sound defense, defenders must not take the bait or commit to the many feints by good forwards. A good dribbler waits for the defender to commit one way, then goes the other. Once the defender lifts one leg or "stabs" at the ball, he loses mobility and thus loses the cat and mouse game unless he gets the ball. Therefore, defenders must employ patience until they can get the ball cleanly, or get help from midfielders or other teammates who will try to steal the ball while the defender covers his man.

How the defender gets the ball is a matter of practice, confidence and instinct. The simple cat and mouse game trains defenders to use their feet and mobility, as well as honing their instinct and tackling skills. A tackle in soccer means trying to get the ball, preferably while staying on both feet. Slide tackles are spectacular and often effective, but they are mostly desperate measures to get to the ball in the defensive end. When a defender leaves his feet to slide tackle a ball, he loses mobility, and unless he gets the ball, he's out of the play until he recovers again. With repetition and practice young defenders can improve their ability to make good tackles, and can improve their tackling "range" and style.

When a defender makes his move is a matter of good instinct and different scenarios. In one scenario: The ball is passed to an attacker on the wing, the outside back cuts him off in midfield. They're both isolated, and the attacker has good control of the ball. Should the defender try to make a tackle or dispossess the

Proper one-on-one defensive coverage. Note the lowered center of gravity on the defender. He is watching the ball and is not going for the various body fakes from the attacker. Also, note his staggered stance that invites the attacker toward the touch lines.

With his poke tackle unsuccessful, the defender has gambled and lost! The attacker takes advantage of the defender's mistake and calmly goes by.

A perfect illustration of using the touch line as a friend. The defender has successfully pushed the attacker out toward the line where his progress ends. The attacker has nowhere to go but backwards!

opponent? The coaching answer to this is "no." The defender is better off covering the attacker and waiting for his teammates to react to the flow of the play. Players must remember that unlike American football, soccer is not a game of inches or possession, therefore, they must rely on patience and good judgement. The attacker on the outside midfield is not a threat to score, but if the defender misses the early tackle, he may allow the opponent to roam free down the wing or middle to make a clean unobstructed pass for a scoring chance. The lone defender is better off covering and waiting for a teammate to challenge for the ball (unless he can positively make a play for the ball himself).

This series shows one-on-one coverage for about 15 yards. Note how the defender has contained an excellent dribbler without committing for a tackle without help. By peddling backwards, he has kept the distance between him and the defender constant. This defensive patience usually pays off by frustrating attackers and allowing secondary defenders to help out.

In another scenario, the ball is passed from midfield through the middle behind the central defenders, and a fast forward pounces on it and breaks through. What should the outside back do? In many instances such as this, outside backs may have a better angle to play the ball than the central defenders. This could quickly turn into a scoring chance and the outside back that anticipates or sees this play must chase down the forward and try to make a play or a tackle.

A common rookie mistake. A defender goes for the fake and the ball without support. The result is always the same for any decent dribbler.

A third scenario has an attacker barely squeaking past the outside back on the wing, but the back quickly recovers. As the attacker tries to reconciliate his advantage, the back recovers quickly and runs back to *reestablish* the inside position. The back uses his speed without the ball, and succeeds in gaining the inside line once again. The cat and mouse game starts again, and the back succeeds in containing the attacker until he gets help from teammates.

In other words, defenders must quickly judge different situations and rely on their speed and ability to make a play. Individual abilities may greatly influence the style and methods used in covering or stealing the ball. Defenders in general, however must remember that soccer is a team sport, and patience usually pays off in getting help from teammates who can aggressively try to steal the ball while they (defenders) protect the imaginary inside line. This doesn't mean that defenders never try to take the ball away from an attacker. They must do this whenever possible but must not create more problems by gambling on 50/50 tackles and allowing attackers to roam unmolested after that. Playing cat and mouse to its fullest is a staple of good outside defense, and it often frustrates attackers who are adept at going past aggressive defenders who gamble early and often.

Another useful tactic for outside backs is using the sidelines to help them contain and stop attacks down the wings. The sidelines are the defender's friends most of the time, and a good outside back can use them advantageously. By pushing opponents toward the sidelines, defenders can narrow the area they need to defend considerably and force attackers to make highly predictable moves. Also, although there are instances when an outside back may pass inside, young backs are taught never to pass to the middle in the defensive zone, especially in traffic or under duress. These passes frequently turn the ball over to the other team in a dangerous part of the field and must be avoided whenever possible.

Finally, although being able to head effectively is a very favorable defensive skill; outside backs don't have to be the tallest and strongest headers on the team. This privilege belongs to the tougher and taller inside defenders. A well-rounded outside back, however should practice heading the ball and clearing it whenever possible, especially when challenged inside the box.

Although outside backs have traditionally been agile, small to medium-size players who can cover their speedy opponents on the wings, many taller players have excelled in this position lately. Tall Paolo Maldini of the legendary AC Milan and Italy is probably the best left back to play the game in the Nineties. His Brazilian counterpart Roberto Carlos who plays his club game at Real Madrid is one of the best attacking outside backs. This diminutive Brazilian is known for his deadly free kicks, and his frequent forays into the attack. Other great outside backs from the past include Paul Breitner and Berti Vogts, who played left and right back respectively for the 1974 World Cup-winning West German team. Vogts, a hard working prototypical back coached the German team at the 1998 World Cup in France, and recently resigned after disappointing results.

Playing Central Defense

*P*laying defense in the middle is quite different than playing outside. Central defenders don't have the luxury of time that outside backs and all other field players may have. A forward inside the box can pounce on a ball and turn it into a goal in the blink of an eye. Therefore, central defenders must make saving tackles and clearances with obvious urgency. Rather than turning the penalty box into a continuous fire drill, however, experienced defenders can avert most dangerous situations by playing a smart and organized game. This usually means anticipating all attacks and dangerous plays before they happen, and positioning themselves for routine interceptions of the ball in the air or on the ground.

The fact that scoring is low in international and professional games is due to the proficiency of these teams' individual and team defense. Central defenders must play the position at all times. Subsequent chapters of this book will cover defensive tactics that include playing the offside trap and other team defensive measures. Fundamentally, however, central backs must try to clear every ball before or as soon as enters the box.

In today's game, a great number of thrusts into the box take the form of crosses from the wings or elsewhere. The central defenders' primary duty is to challenge the results of these crosses in the air and on the ground before the opposition can reach them. These aerial and ground battles can be brutal, and if one keeps track, the tougher and well-positioned defenders usually win most of these challenges. The problem is that most good forwards need one or two perfect opportunities per

Close marking is a useful and common practice in central defense.

game to score. This is perhaps why playing central defense demands more perfection than any other field position. Based on this, central defenders must be strong challengers, and must practice the fundamental, subtle (and sometimes gruesome) aspects of winning aerial and ground duels inside their box.

To do this, defenders must first learn to head the ball unchallenged, and any form of practice is helpful in this regard. This includes a variety of exercises, especially crosses from the corner spot or the wings. As part of team practice, midfielders cross the ball, attackers can try to convert the crosses, and defenders attempt to clear. With proper ground rules, all can improve their skills with minimum contact and no serious injuries.

Contact in the air is largely unavoidable when challenging for headers, and this is usually advantageous for defenders who are, normally tougher than most players are. In fact, a fundamental aerial defensive skill requires initiating contact with a forward in mid-air to prevent him from heading the ball cleanly. This is especially true if the defender cannot be the first to the ball, and the attacker has a better position to

Playing central defense isn't for the feint hearted!
Defenders must contest every ball, and fight aerial duels
with hungry and skilled forwards.

Becoming a Soccer Player

play it. The contact in question has to be legal of course and it usually consists of adding the defender's weight to the attacker's in mid-air, which ensures disrupting the header's timing.

Now that we described *what* center backs do, we will explain *how* they do it. Just as their outside teammates, central defenders must also play the imaginary inside line. Excluding the offside trap, center backs must not allow forwards behind them, and must do all they can to reestablish the inside position at all times. The same judgment that prevails on the outside also applies inside regarding making a quick decision to cover or challenge. It takes good deal of coaching and experience to learn the subtleties of defending one-on-one or defending a zone. The best advice to give young defenders is to simply stay "inside" their opponents, and never allow them to gain the advantage (notwithstanding soccer's fluid offside line).

This takes vision, discipline and perseverance. Note that all of these are mental, not physical attributes! As the other team attacks, central defenders must closely watch the progress of the ball and opponents away from the ball. This *vision* allows them to anticipate the opposition's next move and determine the best strategy for retreat or interception. The defenders' *discipline* prevents them from making rash decisions, or from trying to take the ball away before it is attainable. It also keeps them from straying outside their crucial position, and to stay inside where the real danger looms. Central defenders may of course make plays outside (on the wings), but since they are inside specialists, it is best they stay inside whenever possible. Outside backs and midfielders are better off defending on the flanks, keeping the crucial inside plays to the center backs.

Perseverance is a good trait for all athletes, and defenders are no exception. If they lose a challenge or a position to an opponent, they must never give up! By following each play until its conclusion, they can reestablish position, help their teammates, and save goals even at the goal mouth.

A player may have all the mental attributes and toughness to play defense, but without the proper skills, he or she can be a defensive liability. Some of the required skills to play defense include running backwards while watching the play, being able to make good contact with the ball with the head or the feet, and the ability to extend the body to kick or slide-tackle the ball. The most fundamental of these is making contact with the ball, and defenders should practice this as much as possible. Heading the ball may actually be an easier skill since the head presents a larger target. Contacting the ball with the foot and kicking it out of danger requires good timing and practice.

One of the best drills to develop this valuable skill is having teammates send in various kicks and crosses and letting the central defenders contact and clear them. The key to making clean contact with the ball is timing, watching the ball, and adding force to the kick the moment *after* contact is made. If a player swings at the ball before it reaches his foot, he may miss it completely. Additionally, it is better in many instances to use the inside of the foot to contact the ball rather than the top. This simply presents a larger surface area for the ball to land on.

Different Defensive Roles

*M*ost soccer enthusiasts have heard the various terms describing the different roles of center backs. These include the sweeper, stopper and man-marker. Any experienced player can adapt to these defensive roles depending on available personnel and the defensive alignment. In simple terms, the sweeper is the last man back who ideally does not commit early, and positions himself for the last possible tackle or play. The stopper on the other hand tries to stop or intercept the play earlier knowing that if he misses, the sweeper is there to stop it. The two roles (and players) are interchangeable and flexible. Ideally, it takes good communication between the two to ensure good defensive coverage.

The man-marker is not a traditional position, but many teams that have recently strayed from the back four (using four backs) have adapted a man-marker and sweeper system. In other words, having one or more defensive players with good one-on-one skills to mark opponents. In many instances the marked players are the opposition's best strikers or midfielders who may be frustrated or shut out by the continuos coverage.

Regardless of formation and roles, the key to good defense is the individual and team performance of the players on the field. A coach may have the perfect alignment and roles outlined, but if the defenders make several fundamental errors, even the best strategy cannot help. Therefore, defenders in general must learn how to play defense and practice their skills continuously. Learning strategy and roles can follow.

Playing team defense is an important aspect of the game, and to do so, the defensive unit must have cohesion and good communication. This won't work well unless the individual players understand their roles and abilities. The more players know each other (to the point of liking and respecting one another), the easier it is to play in unison and help each other faithfully. The goalie can also be part of this unit, and it is the duty of the backs (especially the central backs) to help and cover the goalkeeper whenever possible. A good example is to cover rebounds quickly and prevent attackers from pouncing on them. Likewise, the goalkeeper can help his defenders through constant communication and play calling. This is especially helpful since goalkeepers can face the play most of the time, and therefore may have a better vision than defenders who are constantly moving. Subsequent sections of this book will cover team play in better detail.

One of the most basic and important skills associated with playing team defense involves having the first defender cover and delay the ball's progress. This allows other defenders (sometimes called second and third defenders) to provide support and organize the defense behind the first defender. The second (or supporting) defender may actually call defensive plays by telling his teammate to try for the ball, or to "shepherd" the ball one way or the other. If the first defender is beaten, the second defender takes the role of the first defender and so forth.

As mentioned earlier, some of the world's best players are center backs and sweepers. They all have many traits in common that include mental and physical toughness, as well as a vast amount of experience. There are only a few young sweepers at the highest professional levels, and most are seasoned veterans with enough experience to play this crucial position. Lothar Matthaeus of Germany played in five world cups in his storied career and is still Germany's sweeper as late as 1999. Another well-known sweeper is Franco Baresi of AC Milan and Italy fame.

Matthaeus was originally a rangy midfielder who ran the offense and controlled the game before moving to sweeper later in his career. Baresi, on the other hand, is the prototypical well-versed Italian defender who played on AC Milan during its dynastic years of the Eighties and Nineties. He captained Italy during its phenomenal run at the 1994 World Cup, and came back from injury to play in the final game against Brazil. The result after overtime remained 0-0, mostly due to Baresi's effective marshaling of an excellent Italian defense. The game's nil-nil result did not diminish from the quality of play on both sides, especially on the well-organized Italian defense. Brazil won that game after a penalty shootout.

The sweeper covers a loose ball in the box.

The Midfield Generals

*T*he tactical history of soccer evolved from an offensive-minded game in the Fifties and Sixties, to a defensively dominated one in the Eighties and Nineties. More recently, the game has shifted its focus to midfield. Very few teams today play with less than four midfielders. The most common professional formation is some form of 4-4-2, which translates to four defenders, four midfielders and two forwards (plus a goalie of course). Modern teams may cut down on attackers and defenders, but they will rarely play with less than four midfielders.

This shift to midfield is due to new tactical thinking, and a desire to have better-rounded players who can attack, defend, as well as control the tempo. After all, movement, whether defensive or offensive in nature has to pass through midfield. Therefore, midfielders have become the game's generalists who perform all tasks and who contest the ball from goalmouth to goal mouth. Defenders, goalies and forwards are specialists, but midfielders can generally do everything required of a soccer player. The ideal midfielder understands the tactical aspect of the game, can defend and attack, and has the stamina and fitness to run a small marathon in every game.

It doesn't take special studies to show that midfielders are the hardest working athletes on the field, aerobically speaking. As the other team gains control of the ball, midfielders pressure the ball and draw the first line of defense. As the ball advances into their territory, and defenders hold the inside line waiting for help, midfielders usually try to strip or steal the ball. If they fail, defenders can cover them. Midfielders can retreat as far as the goal line to help the defense.

Likewise, as the team starts to attack, it is the midfielders that usually move the ball forward, and who add their weight to the outnumbered attackers. France's three goals in the '98 World Cup finals came from midfielders, not from forwards. Its midfield foursome played an excellent tournament and brought home the coveted trophy.

Athleticism isn't enough to make a good midfielder. Other assets include dribbling and fundamental skills, vision, tactical awareness, positional savvy and smarts. The one midfield general who embodied all these traits is Diego Maradona of Argentina. This short, thick-legged, emotional player guided Argentina to a fantastic win at the 1986 World Cup in Mexico. He single-handedly beat two excellent teams in a row, scoring two goals in each game against European powers Belgium and England. Two of these goals were classic Maradona runs from deep in midfield where he dribbled past seven or eight players before finishing with a beautiful goal.

Maradona embodied the skills and vision of a great midfielder. Great dribbling and ball control skills, phenomenal acceleration, accurate well-weighted passes, as well as a great desire to compete and win. He demonstrated his tactical awareness at all times, as in the 1994 World Cup when he beat the still-organizing Nigerian defense with a sudden free kick/pass to his forward who scored. So how do other midfielders stop the world's most talented player? Unfortunately, there was a time when they fouled and harassed him to submission!

Until new FIFA rules came into effect to protect talented players, it was customary for hard-working midfielders to foul their opponents as much as possible to slow them down and take them off their game.

Although most fans frowned upon these tactics, many coaches adopted them to equalize the talent on the field. Luckily, the new rules admonish such behavior and force all players to improve their skill and stamina. Today's midfielders are excellent athletes in great shape that can run nonstop for 90 minutes and more. Midfield is still however, a place where titans clash, especially in the top European and South American leagues, where players must not only be good athletes, but durable ones as well.

Playing outside midfield

*J*ust as on defense, playing outside midfield is different than playing inside. Traditionally, outside midfielders are more offensively minded, and most attacks can materialize better if they start on the wings. Because of this, outside midfielders must also play a defensive role since the opposition's attacks may start on the wings as well. Midfielders are the link between offense and defense, especially on the outside. As an example, if the right midfielder is involved on defense, the left half should stay open for an outlet pass that starts the counterattack.

Likewise, when the other team attacks down the wing, it is the primary duty of that side's midfielder to defend and harass until the ball is repossessed or switched to the other side. Just as outside backs, it is best for midfielders to stay on their side or pinch to the middle if necessary. If the conditions warrant it, however, they may cover any part of the field. Also, it is not unusual for the left and right midfielders to switch during a game for tactical reasons. It helps of course if both can play the opposite wing since traditionally left-footed players play left, and right-footed ones play right.

Since they cover so much ground, outside midfielders should ideally be fleet-footed and rangey athletes who won't run out of gas running up and down their wing. Speed is another good asset to have on the outside, and there's nothing more troublesome than a speedy winger running up and down the sidelines. Other good attributes include the ability to open up for an outlet pass, then turn and start the attack quickly. So is the ability to do something good with the ball after bringing it down the field. A good midfielder can pass, shoot on goal, and best of all, cross the ball cleanly into the middle, thus creating good scoring chances.

One of the primary duties of outside midfielders is crossing the ball. Here a player demonstrates dribbling and crossing. Note how her hips turned to the direction of play at the conclusion of a successful cross.

Skill practice for outside midfielders includes dribbling down the wings and crossing the ball. Coaches can show players how to turn their hips when kicking the ball on the run so they could cross it effectively. If a midfielder cannot cross the ball high in the air, it will be intercepted easily by waiting defenders. Therefore, midfielders should perfect the art of the cross through continuous practice. A couple of tips coaches can emphasize are for the midfielder to penetrate as much as possible down the wing before crossing the ball, and cutting inside the backs that try to block the ball. By penetrating deep before crossing the ball, midfielders can negate the offside call and set up their forwards with easy-to-convert balls. Also, as backs pursue midfielders down the wing, the winger can suddenly stop and turn behind the pursuing back to cross with opposite foot. Drilling these skills several times each practice can improve game effectiveness tremendously.

Like the backs that play behind them, outside midfielders have a lot of room to operate independently at times, and they also run into many one-on-one situations. Because of this, they must establish a good connection with the fullbacks playing behind them. The left midfielder's best friend on the field is often the left back, and the same applies on the right. Those two own their side of the field, and must try to keep it under control offensively and defensively. The midfielder must therefore help on defense, and the back help on offense whenever possible. It is not unusual for the outside backs to overlap the midfielder and cross the ball from deep within the opposition's side. This means the midfielder has to cover defensively while the back is up front. Overlaps also afford midfielders some rest since they usually log more miles on the field than either defenders or forwards.

Outside midfielders must also know how to play with central midfielders and attackers. Playing central midfield is different than outside midfield as we shall see later, but the two positions must play in unison to achieve success. Central midfield could be congested grounds full of hard tackles and challenges. Smart midfielders will often pass the ball outside to their open teammates who can create offensively in less crowded parts of the field. Therefore, outside midfielders must make themselves good targets and outlets for their central counterparts. There's nothing more comforting than looking up from defense or midfield to a wide open teammate waiting near the sidelines for a pass. Good players always move without the ball and position themselves strategically for clearances and passes.

With such emphasis on defense nowadays, all four defenders and both central midfielders will often crowd the box to prevent the opposition from scoring. Depending on the number of attackers, at least one midfielder may stay outside the box to receive a clearing pass and start a counterattack. Many teams today defend with seven or eight players inside the box, especially during corner and free kicks. Regardless of the situation, outside midfielders are the players in the best position to turn defense into offense, and carry the play into the opposition's side of the field. One of the most exciting midfielders to watch today is Ryan Giggs who plays for Manchester United in England. Giggs' abilities to dribble, shoot and cross the ball have made him one of the most enjoyable footballers in the world. Even the talented Giggs would probably be unable to shine or roam as freely in other parts of the field. Outside midfielders, or wingers as some have called them in the past, are still some of the most exciting soccer players to watch.

The Central Links

*B*y virtue of their positioning, central midfielders are the players that can control the game more than any others on the field. In a balanced alignment, the central midfielders are the players operating in the middle of the formation. Most movement, whether defensive or offensive, goes through central midfield. Consequently, central midfielders should see more action than any other players on the field. Based on these facts, this position requires athletes in good physical and aerobic shape, as well as great tactical and game savvy. Central midfielders must constantly change defense to offense, and vice versa. At one point they can defend the goal, and then they can score goals inside the opposition's penalty box.

Great midfielders must have the ability to read the play and control the tempo. They should routinely read plays before they happen, and position themselves to intercept passes all over the field. They can dribble to gain time and space, as well as start the offense with long or short passes. The best can confuse defenses by changing the style or the method of attack. Down the wing one time, long passes the other, and dangerous through balls yet another. It takes an experienced player who can think on his feet to accomplish these tasks, most of which are mental, rather than physical. Players who rush up and down the field without a specific purpose will eventually tire and fade from the game. Instead, tactical awareness and clear thinking are better attributes to ensure controlling the game's tempo. By being more thinkers than "runners," midfielders can pace themselves for the vigorous demands of tough games and long tournaments.

It is common nowadays to have different roles for the central midfielders. Some, based on their talents, are designated as offensive midfielders, while others have defensive responsibilities. In such a formation, the coach may grant the offensive midfielder free reign to attack and create opportunities, while the defensive player is assigned to disrupt the opposition and stifle their offensive thrusts. This popular tactical decision features two teammates with quite different styles. One is a creative player with great dribbling and attacking skills, the other, a hard-working, tough-tackling player with more substance than style. Together, the two make up a balanced midfield capable of controlling and winning games.

Regardless of the formation, central midfielders must understand that their position requires them to be all over the field, and to play closely to all positions. They can pass to the left midfielder at one point, then

Central midfielders are some of the busiest players on the field, always attacking, defending or covering.

dribble down the right wing at another. Minutes later, they may defend the goal in front of the goalie, or help cover the sweeper who ventured into a rare attack. The better their tactical awareness, the better they will play each game.

Many teams live or die based on their central midfielders' performance. The 1986 World Cup was dubbed as the "Maradona Cup" due to Diego's dominance of almost every game in the tournament. Even with strong man marking by the German team in the final game, Maradona, while uncovered once for a blink of an eye, provided the through pass that resulted in an easy game-winning goal in the dying minutes. Other great central midfielders who control the game from their position are Dunga of Brazil and Zidane of France. The two met head to head in the 1998 World Cup final, with Zidane and France winning this duel. Many believed that Dunga's performance was sub-par during the final, but even this fiery leader could not motivate the Brazilian team that started the game in disarray (due to Ronaldo's epileptic seizure before the game, and other factors).

Zidane had a stellar game for his side by scoring two early headers, and by not allowing Dunga to dominate midfield like he had done in previous games. Therefore, tactically speaking, the game was won by the French midfielders who played an inspired game against a disorganized and demoralized Brazilian team. Had Dunga been able to stop Zidane, the favored Brazil would have probably won the cup like they had done in 1994. This memorable game may have symbolically signaled the passing of the torch from Dunga to the younger Zidane as the world's best central midfielder.

Skill practice for central midfielders includes practicing everything from dribbling to passing to heading. Scrimmages may be ideal situations to practice these skills, especially in crowded midfields. Coaches can teach their central midfielders more on strategy, such as passing the ball outside when under pressure, or dribbling the ball in open spaces to gain space and time for their team. Since central midfielders can score goals as Zidane and Maradona have demonstrated through the years, players in this position should also practice shooting and heading the ball on goal during every occasion.

Zinedine Zidane (10) asserts himself as one of the world's best midfielders during the '98 World Cup final in France. Here he scores the first of his two headers against mighty Brazil.

Becoming a Soccer Player

The Snipers

A typical soccer score in the Fifties or Sixties would have been 6-4 or 7-3 as opposed to today's average scores of 2-1 or 3-2. The difference is simply due to modern strategies that employ lesser forwards than in the past, when four or more players played up front. Some attribute the drop in scoring to better defenders and defensive strategies, and others attribute it to a lack of offensive talent today as opposed to past talent. It is obvious that today's defenses are much better organized and professional than ever, but it is totally untrue that the world today has any less offensive talent. Even the great Pele did not have to play against the likes of Maldini and Mathause. Some of the world's most exciting and expensive players today are goal scoring magicians who frequently play up front solo, or with one partner.

In a typical 4-4-2 formation, two forwards share the duties of scoring or creating goals. These forwards, who are also called strikers, may attack from the wing or down the middle, or both. Good forwards possess certain qualities that help them score goals. Primarily, they must make good contact with the ball regardless of its origin. This means that they must be able to direct the ball toward goal whether it is passed high, low, fast or slow. This seems simple enough, but in reality, some players use better techniques for contacting the ball than others do. Other striker qualities include an uncanny ability or instinct to be at the right time and place, otherwise known as opportunism. Speed is also quite useful to a forward, so is physical strength and the ability to shield and turn with the ball inside the box.

Many strikers have traditionally been short, quick players who have the ability to turn defenders inside out with their great dribbling skills. Lately, however, the average forward has grown in size to match the heading capabilities and strength of modern defenders. The player's size does not matter in the end, but may very well dictate his style and ability to make plays in the air or on the ground.

Skill practice for forwards includes shooting, shooting and more shooting! There are many variations to this skill. Beginners can shoot a stationary ball from various angles, but a better exercise is shooting the ball from the dribble, or even making cuts that simulate beating a defender before shooting the ball. Another important drill is crossing the ball to forwards who must convert it on net either with their feet, heads, or any legal part of their anatomy. This particular drill requires good sub-skills that include timing the kick and making sure players make good contact with the ball (as opposed to no contact or miskicks due to bad timing and technique).

Other important skills include one-on-one against defenders, taking penalty shots, and practicing breakaways on goal and finishing. When practicing breakaways, it's important to instruct the goalie and forwards to use their judgement and to avoid collisions. Practice is for improving skills, not for getting injuries, and players must forsake their egos as they try to score or make saves. The best breakaways usually end with the ball chipped over the sprawling goalie, or with the attacker deeking the goaltender and dribbling around him to score. Every forward must have a strength and a plan to finish such an opportunity.

Scoring goals gets the crowd and the team going! The Swedish team celebrates a goal at the 1999 Women's World Cup.

Some of the shooting techniques are outlined in the kicking section of this book, as well in the accompanying photographs. Other than the fundamentals, coaches can also teach forwards some of the tactical considerations when playing this position. Perhaps the most important one is playing and understanding the offside concept. There's nothing more frustrating to a team than having an attack or score negated due to an offside infraction. Therefore, forwards must be drilled with the *idea* to always play onside.

So how does the offside rule work in soccer? Unlike hockey, for example, soccer's offside line is imaginary and moving. But it is simple to grasp: When the ball is passed forward, there must be two opponents between the opposition's goal and all the passer's teammates. The goalie counts as a player, so there must be an additional defender between the passer's teammates and the goal to negate the offside call. This rule is sometimes subject to the referee's judgement and the linesmen's perception. For example, a player may be in line with the defense when the ball is kicked, but the linesman may view it as an offside. Likewise, if the ball is passed forward with a player in an offside position, and this player is uninvolved in the play (i.e. he is trotting back to an onside position and won't play the ball at all), then the referee may allow the play to continue.

Although offsides is subject to some interpretation, forwards especially must understand it and play it accordingly to increase their onside average and decrease offside infractions. Mental discipline and awareness are the best assets to improve tactical and offside awareness, and coaches must train and choose players who possess or can improve these assets. Mental discipline prompts players to think and understand their position on the field at all times, but especially during possible offside situations. These situations increase as the team attacks, and the defense responds by holding its imaginary line. Forwards must be aware of the fluctuations in the defensive alignment to take advantage of the space given to them, or to withdraw to onside positions when appropriate.

Patience is another psychological asset for forwards. By being patient, they won't rush head on toward goal and fall victim to offside traps.

Also, experienced players are patient enough to know that not every play can produce goals or positive results. It takes perseverance and consistency to succeed, and without these attributes, young forwards may hang their heads early if things don't go their way.

Forwards must be able to convert any ball, low or high, toward goal. Note how the attacker accelerates to meet the ball. Since the pass came from his right, the attacker correctly let the ball cross his body and redirected it with his left foot, which in this case is much easier than trying to kick it with the right.

Good forwards play the whole 90 minutes consistently and try to find different venues to score and create chances. This also requires communication with their midfielders and other teammates. They may share information on certain defenders, and try to isolate opponents with two-on-ones to penetrate down the wings. Or they may ask their central midfielders to send through balls down the middle against slower sweepers. This sort of tactical decision making takes place during every professional game.

There will be more on strategy later in this book, but there are some other fundamental aspects to playing forward. These include the ability to shield the ball even from the toughest defenders. Coaches can teach players how to shield the ball effectively by placing the body between the ball and the opponent. Although any player can do this, strength is a great attribute to hold off defenders fighting for the ball. That's probably why some of the most effective strikers today are extremely strong athletes with very muscular and durable legs.

Other fundamental forward tactics include "losing" defenders by drifting away from them at opportune times. Even the best defenders may turn their backs away from forwards while watching the ball's progress. Smart attackers can take advantage of these precious seconds by moving without the ball. This knack for being at the right place and time is not coincidental, but due to good work and technique. So is the instinct for bouncing on rebounds and never giving up on a play. Forwards may be well covered for the majority of a game, but the good ones know how to pounce on opportunities and mistakes, and can often convert them to goals.

An important forward skill involves receiving the ball with the back turned toward goal and shielding the ball from defenders.

Some of the world's greatest forwards include the venerable Pele and his contemporary compatriot Ronaldo. Brazilians don't have a complete monopoly on this position: Gabriel Batistuta of Argentina is one of the top scorers in the tough Italian league, and German Juergen Klinsman also played in Italy, France and Germany before retiring recently. Each of these players has his own style and strengths, and between them they represent the various styles that define the position.

The immortal Pele played in four World Cups from 1958 to 1970, and Brazil won three of them. This very talented player had a typical Brazilian flair, and his style embodied finesse, technique and speed. Ronaldo, who has explosive speed, strength and instinct for scoring, is deadly on the run. He frequently peels off chasing defenders as he uses his speed and strength before clinically finishing with one of his patented low shots. Ronaldo had an excellent 1998 World Cup in France until an epilepsy bout the night before the final game. He rejoined the team hours before the match, and he was not effective in Brazil's surprise loss to France.

Just like Ronaldo, Gabriel Batistuta also plays his soccer in the toughest league in the world in Italy. With incredible leg and body strength, he is one of the toughest attackers to defend against in the air or on the ground. Older than Ronaldo, Batistuta uses his vast experience to move around without the ball and strike suddenly inside the box. American soccer fans may remember Juergen Klinsman for his goal against the U.S. during the 1998 World Cup. While covered one-one-one, he received a long ball inside the box, calmly chested it, looked at the goal, aimed and scored in one fluid motion. Klinsman, a tall German striker, believes in hard work and practice, and he demonstrated the results of his fundamental training throughout his stellar career.

Finally, a description of forwards, or of soccer players in general wouldn't be complete without a mention of the "divine one," as he is known in Italy. Roberto Baggio dazzled the world during Italy's unlikely run toward the final of the 1994 World Cup. He pulled victory out of the jaws of defeat against Nigeria, defeated talented Spain with a last-minute goal, scored both goals to defeat Bulgaria 2-1, and ultimately, played the final against Brazil for a courageous 120 minutes with a tightly bandaged hamstring. It is refreshing to see Baggio still playing in the Italian league despite the fact that most Italian coaches today prefer tougher and stronger players. Having played midfield before, Baggio excels as a withdrawn forward who can start the attack from a deep position. Throughout his career, he has been able to attack from near midfield and finish with beautiful goals and assists.

Players of all experience levels should rent as many videos as possible to watch how the great ones make the game look so simple and beautiful. Peter Schmeichel in goal; Baresi and Maldini on defense; Maradona and Zidane in midfield; Baggio and Ronaldo up front. All these players have exceptional talents and minds for soccer, and they make it all look so easy. It takes one in a million to make a Pele or a Maradona, but if young players were to emulate these stars, the best thing they can do is to work on the fundamentals. It is extremely rare for anyone to see Schmeichel out of position, Maldini fall for a fake, Zidane miskick a ball, or Klinsman miss a trap. All these players became great ones because they initially did the simple things exceptionally well. Tactical thinking and experience can follow.

Chapter III

Strategy and Tactics

- *Playing for Results or Pleasure*

- *Basic Soccer Formations*

- *Team Play*

- *Offside Tactics*

- *Corner Kicks*

- *Free Kicks*

- *Penalty Kicks*

- *Goal Kicks*

- *Throw-ins*

Playing for Pleasure or Results

Soccer is a great way to stay in shape and improve muscular and aerobic shape. The majority of Americans play soccer to stay in shape and enjoy the weekend, not necessarily to compete or improve their skills. While these are noble intentions, this book teaches skills, strategy and tactics even to casual players.

Players must ideally share the same objectives when playing on a team.

One of the most frustrating aspects of recreational league soccer is the lack of organization and skill. Proper organization can help improve the soccer experience, even for those playing for fitness and fun. The first step in organizing a team or a league is deciding on intentions. Should the team organize and play in a high or a low competitive league? What's the skill level of the team or league? How many players should be allowed to join, and should everyone play in every game? Should the team have practice sessions, or simply show up on the weekend to play games? Finally, should the team elect a captain and a coach, or should the organization be left to committee?

Win or lose, the team may reach its objectives by the end of the season.

These are important considerations to address beforehand to minimize confusion and possible disappointment. By addressing these issues and communicating the team's objectives to all participants, players can have realistic expectations, and therefore, they can better enjoy the game.

There is a place for soccer strategy even in a noncompetitive environment. With strategy, players have a guideline to follow, as well as a mental challenge that adds to the psychological enjoyment of the game. Some sort of organization and strategy is essential for teams playing in organized and competitive leagues. These include youth clubs, high school, college and recreational teams.

Basic Soccer Formations

*B*efore a team takes the field, it must have some form of organization, and players must know their assignments and positions. Soccer formations have seen an evolution from offense to defense, and more recently, the game has tilted toward midfield. Teams typically played with more attackers than either defenders or midfielders back in the Forties and Fifties. Brazil's flying World Cup teams of the Sixties and early Seventies popularized the 4-2-4, which featured two halfbacks, as midfielders were known in those days, and four attackers. Two of those attackers were true wingers whose main duties were attacking down the sidelines and crossing or shooting the ball on goal.

To stop the juggernaut of Brazilian soccer and talent, many European teams adapted their strategy to play more defensively in midfield. By adding midfielders, those teams hoped to control the game, and to slow down opposing attacks before they reach their defensive areas. The results of adding midfielders on behalf of attackers were less scoring, and generally speaking, more wins or draws for the teams that used more midfielders. Based on this, the 4-3-3 and 4-4-2 were born. The 4-3-3 formation was widely used in the Seventies, especially in the now defunct NASL. While this formation was less offensive minded than the 4-2-4, it still did not offer the coverage that could snuff out the opposition's attacks in midfield. The 4-4-2 thereafter became the formation of choice in modern soccer.

The majority of professional soccer teams today (especially in Europe) use one version or another of the 4-4-2. Basically, 4-4-2 means playing with four defenders, four midfielders, and two forwards. This sounds simple enough, but coaches regularly make adjustments in this formation based on theirs and the opposition's personnel. The defensive players, for example can play as a "flat four," which means all four players ideally play as one line without a withdrawn sweeper who plays behind, and has the duty of pulling the offside trap. The defenders in this formation should try to keep an intact offside line (which we will discuss later in this book) by being aware of each other's positioning, and should share the duties of sweeping the ball behind their lines.

Another variation of the back four is playing two outside backs, a stopper in the middle, and a sweeper who plays behind the stopper. Although duties may get blurred in a game, the sweeper is the last man in this defense, and ideally is the last man in the defense. By stepping forward to rejoin his line, the sweeper can be a one-man offside trap, which theoretically is much easier to pull than with the whole line advancing forward. Whether a team plays a flat four or a sweeper/stopper formation largely depends on the available talent and experience in central defense.

The outside backs' duties in the 4-4-2 are much better defined. Both backs on either side must contain the opposition's attacks down the flanks and prevent deep penetrations by opponents. Their duties also include preventing unhindered crosses and helping down the middle whenever necessary.

The four midfielders in the 4-4-2 share defensive and offensive duties, as well as taking part in dominating play in the middle. Just as on defense, the formation may call for a flat four with zonal responsibilities, or for a special formation based on personnel. Many teams employ a central midfielder as a defensive specialist or screen to choke the all-important middle attacks by the opposition. Dunga of Brazil and more recently Chris Armas of the U.S. have successfully played that role for their respective teams. This defensive minded midfielder can also attack whenever possible, and since he wins many balls in midfield, he can frequently start the offense with a release pass as Dunga has demonstrated throughout his career.

With a defensive minded player minding the middle, coaches also employ offensive midfielders down the middle and the wings. Maradona may be the best-known attacking midfielder, but young Claudio Reyna of the U.S. is one of the best Americans to play an attacking midfielder within any formation. Attacking midfielders have excellent dribbling and passing skills, as well as excellent vision to serve dangerous balls to forwards and others. Other central midfielder duties include helping the central defenders, especially when the opposition adds numbers to the attack.

The outside midfielders in the 4-4-2 are the marathon men and women of professional soccer. These players must constantly defend against their counterparts, as well as launch
attack after attack down their respective sides. Since the wings are usually less crowded, much of the outside action takes place at high speeds requiring pace and endurance. Outside midfielders must also work closely with the outside backs to prevent quality crosses and chances from the wings.

The two forwards in the 4-4-2 have two clearly defined tasks: score and set up goals. The two players can split the field according to their favored foot, and they can play inside, outside, or float on top of the box or anywhere they feel is best for good results. Since most goals are

Graphic Not to Scale

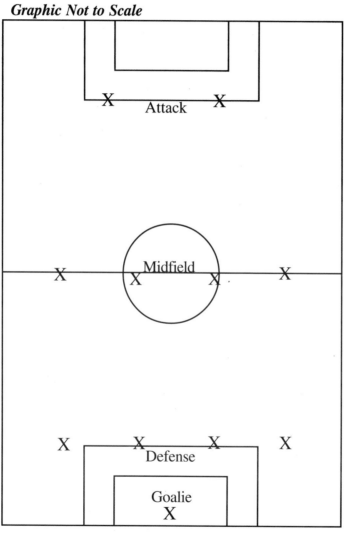

A typical 4-4-2 formation

scored from inside the penalty area, the two forwards must be good finishers and good targets in front of goal. Occasionally, however, they may play outside to draw the defense with them and create opportunities inside for overlapping teammates.

Most professional teams today play some version of the 4-4-2, but there are many squads that are playing with more midfielders at the expense of forwards and even defenders. One such plan is the lone striker plan, or 4-5-1. This particular formation relies on midfielders to control the middle, win the ball, and add attacking weight to a spearhead player who isn't afraid of playing alone and scoring goals. Fans may be the greatest critics of such a formation that limits scoring responsibilities to one player. But with the right personnel, this alignment can be very effective in controlling the game and winning with one or two goals.

Yet another formation used today is the 3-6-1, which uses the most midfielders to gain supremacy. This formation works best with excellent midfield athletes who can cover the whole field and truly defend, attack and play midfield as part of their duties. The six midfielders must add their weight to the depleted defense to prevent opponents crowding the three defenders, as well as attacking with the lone forward to score goals.

Another three-defender alignment is the 3-5-2, which usually relies on a strong defensive midfielder to support the defense. The other midfielders and forwards have similar duties to those players playing in a 4-4-2 formation. The 3-5-2 is probably one of the most preferred deviations away from the 4-4-2 today, especially with the right personnel in midfield. In this formation, a sweeper plays with two strong man markers on defense; the midfielders must clog up the middle and drop back to help the defenders whenever an attack takes place.

The 3-5-2 is gaining popularity because most teams usually play two forwards, so the two man markers and sweeper may take care of the defense while the midfielders try to control the game and win it from midfield. With such firepower behind them, the two forwards can expect good support and many scoring chances to come their way. The reason why the 4-4-2 is still more popular than the 3-5-2 is the fact that four defenders are *assigned* to defend, which psychologically and realistically makes them better defenders than the midfielders who do this as part of their assignment. With more defenders at work, it is obviously harder for the opposition to score or create chances.

The differences between the 4-4-2, the 3-5-2 or any alignment for that matter may lie with the personnel at hand. Interestingly, however, the field's size and opposition's tactics may also contribute to the choice of formation. With a narrow field, for example, it may be difficult to play with more than four midfielders. Likewise, with only a few experienced defenders, a coach who normally favors the 4-4-2 may find it necessary to play a 3-5-2 instead. Whatever the temptation or the circumstance, however, coaches and players must resist the temptation to play with less than 3 defenders, or to experiment in games before practicing a certain alignment. The results of such experimentation are usually sound defeats without accountability. After all, how can a player be accountable for playing in an alignment he's never seen or practiced before?

Graphic Not to Scale

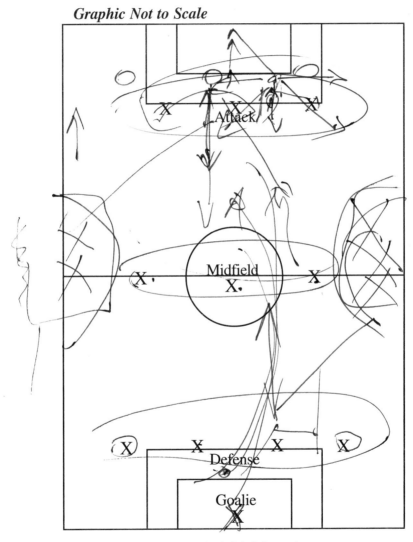

A typical 4-3-3 formation

Team Play

Soccer is a true team sport that relies on team strategy, cooperation, tactics, emotions and morale. For a team to succeed (regardless of whether this success is measured in wins or fun), the players need to practice together, communicate clearly, help each other, and even care for each other. Even the world's greatest players, including the amazing Pele and Maradona played on great teams, and relied upon their teammates for assistance and support. Without team support, the game fizzles, and it won't be fun or productive.

Coaches can talk about and foster team identity, but it is up to the players to preserve and practice it on and off the field. Some players are excellent leaders, and it's very advantageous to have mature captains who can lead by example and help players mesh into the system. One of the team's first acts should be electing or choosing a captain who is well liked by a majority of the players. The captain does not have to be the team's best or most skilled player, but it helps to have experience, maturity and character for this position. The captain's duties include leadership on and off the field, communicating with the players and coaches regarding practice and schedules, as well as helping new and inexperienced players blend into the system. Other traditional duties include talking to the officials, handling the coin toss, and other official business.

Once the team takes the field, it must always display unity and team spirit. It takes time to mesh the different styles and personalities together, so patience is a virtue. Coaches and captains are better off waiting for an opportune time to teach the game, and not try to coach on the fly during a match. The best advice can take place after a game or during practice, and it's best to keep game feedback to positive remarks and encouragement. This is especially true of recreational leagues where players aren't paid to perform, but they pay to have some weekend fun.

In other words, team leaders, including coaches and players must put the team's situation in perspective. If the team and players desire to win every game, they can be pushed harder. If, on the other hand, the objective is to have some good clean weekend fun, then players will probably appreciate any technical advice, but won't accept too much pressure. In the end, the majority will prevail and each team will achieve its goals, no matter how modest or high.

Once the team decides to play together, players will find (or be assigned) their roles and positions on the field. A common mistake in soccer may be to put the weakest players on defense. Any team alignment must start from the back up to the front for good results. This doesn't mean assigning the best striker to play central defense, but rather inserting good comfortable players on defense. Inexperienced players will be exposed early on defense, leading to goals for the opposition and early disappointment for the team. It is actually best to insert beginners as subs at forward and midfield positions, where mistakes cannot be magnified as much as on defense.

When a game starts, the safe strategy is to prevent the other team from scoring early, and from attacking freely. To do this, the midfielders must concentrate on shutting down their opposition and preventing too many unchecked attacks on their defense. The team can then probe the opposition's defenses, especially down the wings, and pick on weak points for further exploitation. There is nothing more inviting to an attack than a weak outside back that cannot control his wing. A smart team will send their best players against the opposition's weakest links to create scoring opportunities. Likewise, the team must watch for uneven situations on defense and help isolated defenders anywhere on the field.

The two best women's teams (the U.S. and China) line up for the World Cup Final in Pasadena, CA. The strategy for both teams was simple: play hard in midfield and don't give the other team many chances. The 0-0 tie after 120 minutes was reminiscent of the men's final between Italy and Brazil in 1994.

Experienced teams know how to read and influence the "flow" of the game. For example, if the team scores first, it can try to play a ball-possession role to frustrate the opposition, spread them out, and open them up for more attacks. Likewise, if the opposition scores first, or they're ahead late in the game, the team must pick up the pace and try more attacks to score. This sense of urgency or casualness manifests itself best in out of bounds and dead ball situations. The team that is ahead usually takes its time in taking throw-ins, corners and free kicks, while the team that's behind tries hard to keep the momentum going. Goalkeepers are some of the best tempo controllers on the field. They can either toss or punt the ball immediately, or take their time bouncing or dribbling it before releasing it.

While these time management tactics are common in advanced soccer, players must be careful not to receive yellow caution cards for time wasting. Referees will only allow some gamesmanship on the field, so players must try to play out their strategy smartly while skirting the tolerance level of the referee. Gamesmanship, however, must not infringe on sportsmanship. Fouling better players intentionally (through tackles) to slow them down or intimidate them is both cynical and dirty, and will earn the culprits yellow or red cards. This isn't to say that smart players cannot use gamesmanship to even out the speed and skill levels against opponents. Tugging on a shirt doesn't hurt players, and most referees who see this infraction will whistle fouls or grant the advantage, but won't necessarily issue a yellow card for the first offense (grabbing a player's shirt to slow him down on a breakaway may warrant a quick yellow, though).

FIFA rules allow for three substitutions during a game. Many leagues around the country have their own substitution rules that allow more players to be substituted. This is especially true of recreational leagues that sometimes allow unlimited substitutions. This liberal policy allows anyone who signed up for the team a playing opportunity. Many players cannot make it to every recreational game, so it is a good idea to have up to 21 players signed up for a season to account for injuries and absenteeism.

Recreational coaches should use most of their players, especially early in the season to keep the players involved, and to help these players grow. If the team is more interested in winning than in equal playing time, the coach/captain should explain this fact to the subs that must accept their roles as support players, especially late in the season. A good analogy to use is the fact that even highly paid professionals sit on the bench, sometimes for a whole season. This may be hard to justify to a player who pays money to play recreational soccer, but playing in scrimmages and practicing with the team may satisfy some beginners who make good subs.

Regardless of playing times and objectives, players and coaches must communicate these objectives to ensure harmony and success. Many recreational players join leagues to meet people and make friends, so they may be satisfied to get a little playing time. The team can truly bond together off the field through social events, dinners, and so forth. As players know each other better, they will also mesh on the field and will communicate and cooperate more freely.

Teams playing in high school and college leagues have an easier time of managing subs and choosing the best starters for each game. The focus can shift toward winning strategies and tactics based on available talent and competition. Coaches can insert their subs accordingly to rest tired

Strategy and Tactics

players, or to finish lop-sided games where playing the starters becomes futile or unnecessary. Regardless of the objectives, soccer can best be enjoyed if played by cohesive and organized teams that encourage communication and camaraderie between all players.

Offside Tactics

*O*ne of the most important team tactics involves maintaining a cohesive and effective offside line. This involves instilling the necessary discipline and organization within the defensive unit, as well as practicing the concept on the field through drills and scrimmages. The concept is quite simple: All defenders should ideally form a straight line across the field so not to allow the opposition to go behind them in an onside position. It only takes one defender behind the line to allow the opposition to sneak in. Theoretically, this defender can be on one side of the field, and the opposition may penetrate the other side without being offside because of that defender's position. It is important to note that a player cannot be offside in his own half of the field, so the offside rule only applies when an attacking player is in his offensive side of the field.

Teaching individual defenders to play in line to maintain the integrity of the offside line can be quite simple with the right personnel, and time-consuming with others. A young player may fully understand the concept and how to stay in line, but may stray repeatedly and ruin the offside. Therefore, a team should practice its defensive alignment and offside tactics whenever possible. Coaches and experienced players can help young defenders by constantly reminding them of their position on the field. Ideally, the sweeper is in perfect position to organize and observe the defensive alignment.

The sweeper, goalie or any player can "call" the line to move forward to trap the opposition in an offside position, or to prevent them from penetrating deeper without the ball. This call to move the line forward is most effective after the ball is cleared from the defensive box. If defenders don't move up, the opposition can kick the ball right back to the dangerous box and play it. If the line moves up, a forward pass may find the opposition trapped offside, thus saving a potentially dangerous situation.

China maintains a perfectly straight offside line during a U.S. free kick. Note how the U.S. attackers (in white) remain onside until after the kick is taken.

Graphic Not to Scale

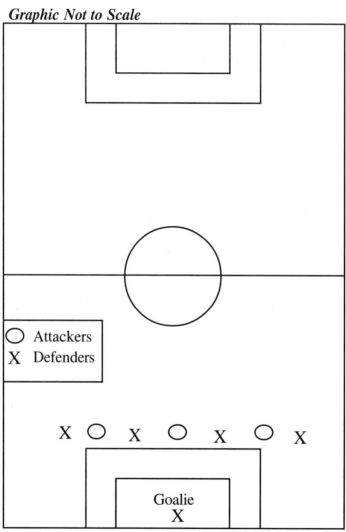

Attackers ○
Defenders X

X ○ X ○ X ○ X

Goalie
X

The forwards in this diagram are onside

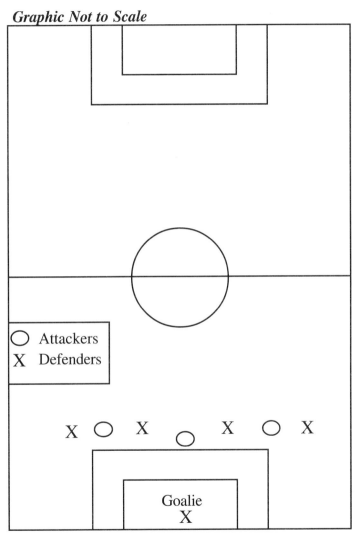

Graphic Not to Scale

Attackers ◯
Defenders X

Goalie
X

In this example, the forward in the middle is in an offside position

Finally, another method to play the offside trap involves one key player, such as the sweeper who can pull it at the right moment. In this case, the sweeper plays behind the other defenders who keep a straight line between them. Opposing forwards may fill the gap between the sweeper and the rest of the defense, and if he times it right, the sweeper can advance himself to the rest of the line, and cause the opposition to withdraw back or to be left offside. This "sweeper trap" is easier to pull since it involves one player making a single decision, rather than the whole line acting in concert.

Playing an offside strategy requires having experienced players since it can be risky. Risk, however, has its rewards at times, and teams that don't have a defensive offside strategy usually play the whole game on their heels since they can surrender territory quite easily. Having a reliable defender that understands and runs the offside strategy can be priceless in modern and advanced soccer.

Corner Kicks

*E*very soccer match has a number of "dead ball" situations, many of which result in goals or dangerous plays. A dead ball is defined as a stationary ball ready to be kicked, such as a corner, free kick or penalty kick. Teams must prepare and practice for these situations from an offensive and a defensive perspective.

The corner kick is one of the most common kicks in soccer. A team earns a corner kick when the other team puts the ball out of bounds through the end line. There was a time in soccer when many equated a corner kick with having earned "half a goal." Those days of weak defense and strong attack are over, however, and many games go on without scoring off of corner kicks. The last World Cup Final game in France, however, was a strong demonstration of the importance of corner kicks, as French midfielder Zidane scored two brilliant headers off of two first-half corners.

Those two corners serve as perfect examples of what to do offensively, and what to improve upon defensively. In the first corner, Zidane practically ran unopposed to meet the ball in the air, with Brazilian Leonardo too late to stop him in the air. Leonardo was not at fault since Zidane, who wasn't his man, originally did not have a marker, and Leonardo realized the danger too late. In the second goal, the stronger and taller Zidane shoved the formidable Dunga to the ground on his way to a similar brilliant run and header. Replays showed that Dunga had been fouled, but unless the referee sees and calls it, it's not a foul! The distracted and disorganized Brazilians had let their guard down twice and did not check the dangerous Zidane as he ran unopposed *before* he made contact with the ball.

As usual, we will start with the defensive assignments. First, both posts have to be protected to help the goalie, and allow him the freedom to roam ahead to punch the ball in the air. Traditionally, two shorter defenders or midfielders can each take a post to allow the taller players to contest the ball inside the box. The center back or marking back should mark the opposition's best player closely, and should not allow him the inside track or a clean run or jump. In other words, any legal contact and "body weighting" is helpful to take the attacker off his stride and force him to make "unclean" contact, or no contact with the ball. Young players should learn how to contest headers by jumping with the attackers and leaning on them in mid-air using legal contact to ruin the attacker's chances of getting clean shots. Headers require precision to be on target, and the slightest contact can usually ruin this precision. Anyone who watched the replays of Zidane's two strong headers can see that he wasn't challenged before getting to the ball, or at the point of contact.

Since even world-class players can be beaten, it is essential for the defending team to have more bodies inside the box than the opposition has. Therefore, the defense must have one man on each attacker, plus at least one or two free players to support the ball and beaten teammates. One of those free players could be the sweeper who is normally a specialist at reading the play and being the last man in. This obviously requires most or all of the midfielders to play defense depending on how many men the attackers employ. The goalkeeper is the great equalizer in a corner kick, and he can outreach anyone using his arms to punch or grab the ball. Therefore, an essential duty of central defenders is to protect the goalie from interference or contact while he concentrates on his tasks.

The goalie and his defenders must also communicate clearly, especially if the keeper decides to go up for the ball, and he should yell to let his teammates know this. He can usually yell "KEEPER," or, "ME," or any agreed-upon or recognizable audible. Regardless of the communication method, goalkeepers must not hesitate when they go for the ball, since any slip-up could result in an opportunistic goal. This is why proximate defenders must retreat back to cover the goal once their keeper goes up to play the ball.

Finally, although the majority of corner kicks are crossed into the box, some teams may employ different tactics or trickery and use a short pass to dribble the ball in. The outside back on that side must read and defend this play with assistance from his side's midfielder. These fluid situations may not seem as dangerous at first since the ball isn't crossed immediately, but their unpredictability may throw the defense off.

Many teams have preset offensive strategies and plays for their corner kicks. These include having designated kickers to take the corner from either side, as well as designated target players who are especially strong in the air. One can surmise that Zidane was a designated target on the French World Cup team, and if he was well covered, the kicker could have picked a secondary target.

Many inexperienced kickers will inadvertently send the corner kick behind the net or within the goalie's reach. A kick that lands out of bounds is a total loss; one that ends up near the goalmouth has very little chance of offensive success with any competent goalkeepers around. Therefore, the best strategy is to kick the ball slightly out of the goalkeeper's range and inside the box for a maximum chance of convergence. If the team has an efficient target player, he should line up near the top of the box to attack the ball inside the box as Zidane did in the 1998 World Cup Final. Other players should spread out to play the ball if it sails too short or too long, or to clean up in front of net.

How many players should get involved in a corner kick depends on the team, score, and available talent. A team behind by a goal with a minute left should probably involve all 10 players including the goalkeeper in the box to try and gain the equalizer. A team ahead by a couple of goals may have no more than three or four players involved inside the box plus the kicker. The players on the field should judge the situation and play the corner accordingly based on their experience and preparation.

Some teams employ specific plays during corner kicks, such as having relay players on the short or far side who head the ball into the middle for finishers. The near post players usually present a more immediate danger since they may be closer to the ball than the defenders, and therefore they may flick the ball unhindered to their teammates. The ball would have to traverse most of the defense, however, to reach a player stationed on the far post, but this can also present a good scoring chance. Regardless of what tactics a team uses, corner kicks should be part of any lengthy practice, and an integral part of team strategy. Coaches can designate kickers and targets for either side of the field based on practice results and observations.

Sweden (in light colors) defends a corner against China at the WWC. Note the good coverage on all the chinese forwards, and the location of the goalie at the extreme right.

Free Kicks

A free kick is awarded to a team when a player is fouled or the ball is handled outside the box. There are two kinds of free kicks: direct and indirect ones. A referee may award an indirect free kick if he redeems the infraction as unintentional. An indirect kick means the ball cannot be kicked directly into the net, but must be touched by a second player before going in. The majority of free kicks however, are of the direct variety, which means the ball may be kicked directly into the net.

Direct free kicks are some of the most dangerous plays in modern soccer, and many teams today have elevated free kicks to a scoring art. Brazilians were the first to score goals in bunches off of free kicks, but European teams soon caught up. Romania and Gheorghe Hadji put on a clinic on free kick scoring during the 1994 World Cup in the U.S. Yugoslav players are some of the best free kick specialists in Europe, and many of them today convert free kicks on premiere Italian and Spanish teams.

So why do some teams or players have great success with free kicks? Simple: they train to score on free kicks, and they have the accuracy, power and artistry to take these kicks. Defensively, the goalkeeper is the key player in defending a free kick. The keeper must shout instructions to his defensive wall to block a part of the goal, while he covers the other. The defensive wall should start closer to the ball than the allowed distance to give the team the time to set up properly. It is the referee's job to push the wall backward, and the players in the wall should cooperate slowly without earning yellow cards. As they do so, other teammates who are not part of the four or five-man wall can find their defensive assignments next to or behind the wall.

The goalie and defense must pay special attention to an opposition player who plants himself at the end of the wall. This player usually peels off the line as an accurate kick flies through his vacated space. By doing so, the ball is kicked toward the net with the goalkeeper initially screened by that player. The best way to defend this situation is for the defender closest to that player to block the shot as it comes through. In fact, the best way to defend any free kick is for players to sacrifice their bodies at the wall and blocking the shots before they get through. Even the best goalkeepers can be beat once the ball crosses the ball, so it's best that it never does.

The goalie is the most responsible defensive player during a wall-building defensive situation. He must communicate audibly and guide his wall left or right as needed.

Where a team must build a wall, and how many players should get involved largely depends on the location and distance of the ball to the goal. It is ultimately the goalkeeper's responsibility to call the number of players in the wall, and to ensure that his goal is blocked properly on the short side, while he cheats to one side or the other. In the end, it comes down to a duel between the kicker and the goalkeeper. Distance and acute angles are the goalie's allies, while proximity and good angles are the kicker's friends.

Much of the offensive responsibility lies with the free kick taker who is usually a specialist at this. Some teams, such as Spain's Real Madrid have the luxury of two or three excellent free kick specialists. Left back Roberto Carlos is one of the deadliest in the late Nineties, and his patented hard-driven banana kicks go around defensive walls to give many goalkeepers fits. Ideally, a team should have a left-footed and a right-footed specialist to take free kicks from either side of the field. If the ball is right of center, a left-footer has a better chance of bending it in, and vice versa.

The key to scoring on free kicks is getting the ball past the defensive wall. A very hard kick may go through the wall with or without deflecting off of players. A more artistic method involves going around the wall with a bending ball that finishes its arc inside the goal. To do so, the shooter must kick the ball on the side to cause it to bend. Acquiring the skill to bend the ball and put it on target requires talent and lots of practice. Players such as Roberto Carlos and Fernando Hiero of Real Madrid have undoubtedly spent hundreds of hours practicing this all-important skill. Young players can improve this skill best by shooting on goal from various distances, and gaining skill and experience through practice.

The U.S. prepares to take a free kick with two players on the ball to confuse the goalie. Note the U.S. player interfering with the well-constructed Chinese wall and the coverage on all the U.S. forwards.

Penalty Kicks

*I*f corner and free kicks represent dangerous situations, then a penalty kick (PK) is almost an automatic goal. The PK is awarded if an attacking player is fouled inside the box, or if a defender in the same area handles the ball. Defensively, the team has to rely on luck and the goalie's athleticism and instincts to stand a chance of stopping this shot. The goalkeeper in this instant has nothing to lose, and most of the pressure is on the kicker to convert. Therefore, the common technique is for goalies to guess which way the ball is heading, and to dive to that side with a full body stretch.

Some goalkeepers can be quite imposing in goal and they give the shooter trouble deciding which way to go. Many distract the shooter by talking to him before he takes the kick, or by staring him down and trying to read his eyes. Yet, in many instances, technique surpasses mind games. The goalie cannot move before the kick is taken, but he can dive sideways and *forward* to cut down the angle and get a better chance of stopping the ball. Traditionally, most players are trained to shoot the ball low into the corner, so the best percentage is to dive to one side and hope to tip or block the shot.

The goalie's job may be void of pressure considering that nine of ten penalty shots should go in. The real pressure lies with the kicker, but the key is not to feel any strain, and to make the kick as routine as possible. With a little practice, any decent player should be able to put the ball in the corner, but that's not always guaranteed to beat a gifted goalie. Shooters should apply a little power to their shot to beat the goalie to the post, and should also employ some body language deception. If the shooter lines up in a manner that telegraphs the side he's shooting for, the goalie may have a better chance at guessing what side to dive to.

Finally, although most amateur goalkeepers can be beaten with a low strong shot, some tall and athletic goalies may be adept at saving these. This forces players to try and shoot the ball higher into the net to negate the goalie's diving ability. It is not coincidental that some of the world's best-known PK misses have been high shots. This is due to the shooters trying too hard to beat a world-class goalie and missing in the process.

How important are Penalty kicks? Ask the Italian national team that has not lost in regular time in three consecutive World Cup playoffs. The Italians lost on penalty shots in 1990 to Argentina, in 1994 to Brazil and in 1998 to France. It is ironic that a well-drilled Italian squad could not win on penalty kicks. One would imagine that their strategy included shutting out talented teams such as Brazil and France, and beating them from the PK spot. Yet, even the great Baggio in 1994, burdened by a sore hamstring and trying to beat Taffarel, shot high handing Brazil its first World Cup in 24 years.

Baggio is still playing marvelous soccer in 1999 and he remains as one of the most consistent penalty takers in the Italian league. Consistency is probably more important than anything, and players should practice the PK from the spot and try to raise their average to 90 percent or better. This will give them the necessary confidence to convert the PK routinely no matter under what circumstances they attempt it.

A Norwegian player converts a penalty against a fully stretched Brazilian goalie at the 1999 WWC.

Strategy and Tactics

Goal kicks

A goal kick is awarded to a team when the ball goes out of bounds off of an opponent through the team's end line. One can view goal kicks as the beginning of possession or offense, but this isn't always guaranteed. Goal kicks are frequently contested in midfield and are not necessarily won or controlled by the kicking team. Although any player can take a goal kick, it is better if the goalie takes it to allow more players to contest the ball, and to allow the defense to establish an early offside line.

It is better for the goalie to take all goal kicks if possible to allow his team to set up an early defense and an offside line.

Since the team knows the range and kicking habits of their goalkeeper, it is possible to line up in preplanned positions to garner and control the goal kick. Many teams have preset positions, especially on the wings, but it is also common to receive the ball in the middle. If the goalkeeper has an injury, or cannot kick the ball high to midfield such as the case on many amateur teams, any teammate may take the goal kick, preferably a defender.

The opposing team in goal kick situations should learn from the early kicks and anticipate the ball in the "landing zones." The ball can be contested in the air or on the ground, and either team can win possession. Perhaps the most important thing in this situation is not to allow the ball to bounce to a streaking forward who breaks in alone on the goalie. The team should practice goal kicks like any other skill. The back-up goalkeeper and a couple of defenders should also practice this skill in case of injury or suspension to the starting goalkeeper.

Strategy and Tactics

Throw-ins

*T*hrow-ins are awarded when the ball goes out of bounds through the touchline off of an opponent. From a defensive standpoint, throw-ins present a serious challenge in that the offside rule does not apply when a throw-in is taken. Due to this rule, defenders must not let attackers sneak behind them in the defensive zone, and should play them very tight to steal the ball or prevent it from being thrown to dangerous players.

It's always best to throw the ball forward from the defensive zone to avoid potential problems near the box. If the other team intercepts this "vertical" throw-in (a throw-in down the field rather than across), the defender who threw the ball in along with other defenders can be in position to play defense. The same can apply from midfield or up front, but there comes a time when throw-ins can present marvelous scoring opportunities. The scope of these opportunities largely depends on the width of the field and the available personnel. A strong throw-in player can toss the ball into the box for a scoring opportunity on a narrow field. Or in case of wider fields, the team may use a relay header to send the ball into the box.

Teams can practice offensive and defensive throw-in tactics independently, or through game scrimmages. Coaches should also ensure that players know the proper throw-in mechanics. These include keeping both feet on the ground, not violating the touchline, and having the ball above the thrower's head. It is not uncommon for referees to award a throw-in to the other team if a player violates throw-in rules. Also, refs may award a retry if the throw-in never enters the field after it's thrown down the line.

The mechanics of a thorw-in. Note how the ball was thrown over the head with both hands and how the feet never left the ground.

Strategy and Tactics

Chapter IV

Advanced Soccer Skills

- *Understanding Position*

- *Advanced Passing*

- *Dribbling & Vision*

- *Space & Direction*

- *Advanced Kicking Techniques*

Understanding Position

*O*ne of the most evident attributes that describe great players is their simple understanding and adherence to the basics. This understanding goes beyond the fundamental skills, such as trapping and dribbling, but it also encompasses advanced skills and subtleties that make someone a great player.

An advanced (and quite subtle) talent that good players possess is their tactical awareness of their position on the field or around the ball. Tactically speaking, a player must be able to move and choose his position with or without the ball for maximum benefits and efficiency. Technical skill gives this player the ability to accomplish these movements efficiently without losing possession, and without losing track of the prevailing play.

It is very difficult to describe or measure tactical awareness since it is not a technical skill that can be easily observed. This book referred to some tactical considerations in the team play section, but unless the majority of players have sound tactical judgement, the team may not have a good one either. The same rules that apply to a team usually apply to individual players, such as judging the run of the play, making decisions, slowing down or upping the tempo, attacking in force, defending from midfield, etc.

One of the simplest tactical decisions that each player makes hundreds of times each game concerns his position in relation to the ball. Should he be behind, ahead, or level with the ball? Sounds simple enough, but this is a serious decision that many players don't process very consciously, when in fact they must. Since soccer is a very fluid game with ebbs, flows, sudden attacks and a fast-traveling ball, tactically savvy players are frequently trying to analyze and adjust their position on the field. When a coach asks a team to tighten up, he is in essence asking players to play behind the ball. Likewise, when a team decides to open up, they can take more risks, and play level or ahead of the ball from midfield on.

This doesn't mean that a team playing behind the ball should not attack, and vice versa. A player ahead of the ball however is not in an ideal position to defend, and he has to run back to gain defensive position. This tactical adjustment may work, but it may be too late to stop a dangerous play from unfolding. Tactical positioning and timing are entwined, thus the famous saying: "The right place at the right time."

A less subtle skill involves technical positioning. We see professional players doing this constantly in any game as they adjust their body position to open up for a pass or start a dribble. Experienced players frequently make this adjustment as the ball is on the way toward them, and they may peddle backward, or cross the ball's path to receive it in perfect position.

So what is "perfect position," or is there such a thing? There is no simple answer to this question other than combining perfection with fundamental soundness. In essence, all movements and adjustments take place so a player can "face" the direction of play. This is a simple concept to explain: The direction of play means facing the opposition's goal, so a player wants to have the ball in front of him as he faces that goal. This way, he can look up the field, deliver a pass, or dribble in the right direction. By establishing the proper position early (even before receiving the ball if possible), a player can have the advantage of direction and position, giving himself a tactical and technical advantage.

The player on the right has just executed a "turn" after faking to the other side. She is now ready to carry the play in the opposite direction.

Conversely, by receiving the ball while facing his own goal, a player may be pressured by the opposition, and may not be able to turn with the ball or pass it forward. One of the few options available to him in this instance is passing back to a teammate who is facing the run of the play. This is why making early adjustments to receive a pass is so important in a game, and why one of the most important calls one can audible to a teammate is "TURN," which lets the player know that he has time to turn before the opposition "rides his back."

The ability to turn before players hear the dreaded "MAN ON" is an essential technical skill. With a little practice, this becomes quite simple, and some gifted players can do it even with a man on. This skill requires shielding the ball while turning, preferably with the ball on the outside of the foot to maximize the distance from the opponent to the ball. A safer and simpler option whenever possible is to pass the ball backward to an open teammate as we shall discuss later. This naturally requires the teammate to acquire the proper position to receive the pass.

Advanced Passing

Advanced passing encompasses accuracy, but more importantly, the ability to pass in all directions and understand various passing concepts. One of the simplest and most common passes that professionals employ is the back pass. This valuable pass ensures possession and allows a teammate in a better position to make a play. Beginners rarely use the back pass, and they mostly pass the ball forward or laterally, frequently into low-percentage situations. Coaches should teach the principle of passing to the open man whenever possible, which includes making back passes that ensure better ball possession, and consequently better opportunities.

The player on the right has just completed a back pass to her teammate. This clever little pass often confuses defenders and reverses the direction of play instantaneously.

Advanced Soccer Skills

Another simple pass to learn is the return pass. Frequently, the passer can open up as soon as the recipient gets the ball, making a return pass an excellent option for continued possession or attack. The one-two or give-and-go is a return pass that has been used in soccer since the game's inception. Players should learn to use these passes all over the field, not just in the offensive zone. The keys to success in the give-and-go are accuracy and movement. Accuracy is necessary to put the ball on its intended target whether the target is the teammate's feet or an open space that he can run into. Positional movement is necessary for the teammate to open up and accept the pass, or to chase it down an open space. There are no silver platters when it comes to receiving passes in competitive soccer, and players must make an effort to receive even the simplest of passes.

The return pass is especially useful when the competition pressures and chases the ball, thus allowing the original passer a chance to open up again. Without pressure, a passer has the option of making passes in any direction, but more importantly, *at any time*. This means the player possessing the ball can dribble the ball and hold it until a good pass presents itself. In other words, passing to the open man when the player has time simply isn't enough, and this may be a perfect opportunity to make the best pass possible for an offensive chance.

This well-timed pass could be to a teammate streaking down the wing, a through pass down the middle, or a cross from the wing into the box. Regardless of the type of pass, it must be accurate enough to give a teammate a reasonable chance of reaching and playing it. The best passes usually end up ahead of a teammate, not at his feet or behind him, but in any case, the recipient must try to reach a pass before the opposition does. There are coaches who teach "there are no bad passes, just lazy pass recipients!" And some good defenders, we might add.

There are different techniques to deliver a pass. The most common of course is kicking the ball traditionally with the inside or top of the foot. There are, however different techniques that players can use to facilitate a pass, or to hide their intentions. Traditional passes usually telegraph their intent or direction, but various techniques can fool the opposition, and create unexpected good results. These include passing with the outside of the foot, passing with headers, and using heel passes.

A player demonstrates a quick wall pass with the outside of her foot during a two-on-one situation.

Advanced Soccer Skills

Since many good players can dribble the ball on the outside of their foot, they can quickly pass the ball with a quick flick on the outside to a teammate in a parallel or advanced position. These quick flicks are hard to read or defend especially if the passer hides his intentions by not looking at his intended target. Likewise, one of the most exciting and effective passes in soccer is the back-heel pass that usually wrong-foots the defense and creates scoring opportunities. The key to a back-heel pass is vision and awareness of teammate and opponent positioning and direction. Players who can deliver this pass consistently are universally considered some of the best to play the game.

Finally, delivering good passes should not be constricted to a player's feet. The chest, head, thighs and shoulders can all be used to deliver unexpected and effective passes. These are particularly effective since there is very little ball possession before making a pass with the chest or the head. Therefore, as soon as the opponent looks at the passer, the ball is relayed to a teammate who is open for a better play.

Good passing is a cornerstone of advanced soccer, and players should study and practice this important skill whenever possible. Some claim that while passing techniques may improve with practice, passing vision is a gift that may not be developed as easily. While there may be a measure of truth in this, one can also argue that good players can develop and improve through continuous practice and study.

Dribbling and Vision

*D*ribbling a soccer ball is one of the simplest skills for an advanced player. Dribbling effectively during a game and finding open teammates with defenders trying to steal the ball, however, requires great skill, strength and vision. Although speed, acceleration and agility are the greatest assets for great dribbling, any player can improve by working on fundamentals, such as protecting the ball and keeping it close to the body. Mental conditioning is also beneficial in deciding when to dribble and keep the ball, and when to pass it. Many good ball dribblers make the mistake of sometimes dribbling at the wrong time and place. One example is attempting to dribble the ball from the defensive zone during the last remaining minutes of a winning match. Odds are the opposing is pressing hard for an equalizer and trying to steal the ball in their offensive zone. A quick release pass to an open midfielder is a far better decision in this scenario.

The opposite can also be true when players with time in midfield release the ball too early to covered teammates when they may have more time to dribble and create "time and space." This is especially true of a midfielder streaking down the wing unopposed and crossing the ball too early before his teammates reach a scoring position inside the box. If a forward crosses the ball too early, the waiting defenders may play it out safely, or the play may be whistled offside since the ball may travel forward. Using the dribble for maximum penetration, the ball carrier can advance and cross it level or backward to negate the offside and provide good scoring chances.

Advanced Soccer Skills

*A good dribbler can look up and spot opportunities
in other parts of the field.*

In simple terms, good dribblers should carry the ball into the offensive
zone until they spot a great pass, or before the opposition can recover
or steal the ball. When and where they pass the ball is largely a matter
of instinct and teammate cooperation. This means that while a player
dribbles the ball effectively, his teammates must open up by moving
without the ball and finding good positions. Unless the team does that,

even the best dribbles become ineffective, unless of course the dribbler takes the ball and tries to score by himself everytime, Maradona style!

It's tough to tell players that it takes instinct to dribble and play well, so coaches should take some measures to teach good dribbling skills. These include teaching players how to shift position to protect the ball, lowering the body's center of gravity to make easier cuts, and using acceleration to keep up with the ball and lose pursuers. Another neat sub-skill to learn is dribbling while scanning the field and without looking at the ball. Players can attain this advanced skill through practice and using their peripheral vision to locate the ball while they scan the field ahead.

Space and Direction

*U*nderstanding the concept of space and direction also requires using mental awareness and experience. Unlike tangible soccer skills such as trapping and kicking, space and direction are intangibles that great players comprehend and apply each game. Space may be defined as any part of the field, but of course this space fluctuates throughout a game. Direction is not as simple as north and south or east and west, but it also it encompasses varying the tempo, switching sides, and *influencing* direction.

Understanding space includes differentiating between *occupied* and *unoccupied* space. Consequently, this means judging how and when unoccupied space will become occupied, and vice versa. This is an important defensive and offensive talent because if a defender is fully aware of the unoccupied space behind him, he will likely make a better decision to defend it. Likewise, an attacker aware of that space can rightfully exploit it with a through pass that a teammate can run into.

Any good player can easily learn to recognize such situations, so the difference many times lies in who sees what first! If the attacker spots the space before the defender, he can hand his team a momentary advantage with a quick pass. If the defense spots it first, it can change its "stance" into an offside line to prevent forward penetration before the pass, or to a quick reacting defense that can chase down the pass before the opposition gets there. Either case starts with *recognition* of the usable space.

Just as players can see empty space, they must also recognize space "patterns." These change with each team and game, and they may include a team's style or habits, meaning how the defense lines up, or how a team attacks down the field. In other words, one team may allow more space than the next one, and empty first-half space may become quite busy and defended in the second half. Since soccer players aren't coached during a game, they must have the ability to recognize these situations and react to them accordingly. This ability comes with experience and coaching, and coaches should urge their players to "open their eyes" and observe space, not just see other players and the ball.

Recognizing direction takes the same kind of savvy required for reading space. Experienced players know how to move and pass efficiently to change the playing direction. A very common directional decision involves a player facing his own goal as he receives or possesses the ball. This player has the option of turning or passing the ball to a teammate who can better play it. Turning with the ball changes the direction immediately giving the player a better view of the *forward* direction toward the opposition's goal. This sounds easier said than done since a player cannot always turn cleanly with the ball if he is closely covered. This is where teamwork comes in.

Players facing forward must always offer assistance to those who are facing the wrong way by presenting themselves as pass targets. An easy back or side pass can restart the play in the right direction. It is clear that the responsibility in these situations isn't just with the player with the ball, but on his teammates facing the right direction.

Advanced Soccer Skills

The player on the left "peels off" to allow her teammate who is facing in the right direction to play the ball. This is a very subtle and useful skill for advanced players.

Defensively speaking, players can deny their opponents clean turns by applying early pressure, and by cutting the passing lanes to players that can start in the right direction. This pressure is especially effective if applied by forwards on the other team's defenders, possibly forcing them to cough up the ball in their own zone.

Coaches can teach their players how to understand and apply directional play during every game. They can assist this concept through various exercises that involve turning and changing directions. One such drill is having players line up Indian file in two lines facing each other. Players dribble the ball and short-pass it to teammates running in the opposite direction, who in turn passes it to another, and so on. By doing so, players understand the mechanics and concept of changing the ball's direction.

Other skills include players going forward and receiving passes from teammates facing the wrong direction. The player facing the wrong way can receive the ball from a teammate, which he returns right, left and behind him. He becomes the pivot in a string of passes leading forward, and he may employ traditional, side and back passes to deliver the ball to his teammates going forward. Even players facing the wrong way can make great plays by understanding direction and space and using them to their advantage.

Advanced Kicking Techniques

*A*dvanced players can kick the ball in many different ways to pass it through defenders or to beat goalies. The primary variable between different kicks lies with what part of the foot contacts the ball, as well as what part of the ball is contacted. Any part of the foot or the ball may be used to create a kick, and each will have a different effect on the ball's trajectory and velocity.

The most common kick of course is the one using the top of the kicker's foot, commonly referred to as kicking "from the laces." Advanced players can strike the ball on either side to change its trajectory from a straight one to a bending path resembling a banana. These kicks are quite effective in going around defensive walls and other obstacles on their way toward goal. Coaches can show the mechanics of bending the ball to their players who in turn can practice them using obstacles that resemble defensive walls or players.

By striking the ball on its right side with the right foot, the ball will spin and bend toward left. Likewise, if struck with the left foot on the outside left, the ball will bend to the right. Since most players have one dominant leg, they may have to strike the ball differently to change the ball's trajectory. For example, if a right-footed player wants the ball to bend to the right, he must strike it on its left side using the outside of his right foot. These kicks using the outside of the foot are some of the most advanced and hardest to master, so they naturally require a great amount of practice.

One of the most spectacular kicks to execute and watch is the bicycle kick. Interestingly, the primary reason for this kick is making contact with a ball that is *behind* the kicker. Ideally, the ball should be ahead of a player for him to kick or head it, so the bicycle kick is a last resort to kick the ball if the player doesn't have time to control and turn the ball for a simpler kick. The bicycle kick may be executed defensively or offensively, and players who can execute it can provide a thrilling and exciting play. Coaches, however, should explain to their players that bicycle kicks are a lot harder and less accurate than regular kicks, and should be used as a last resort. Ideally, players should try to execute their kicks while facing the goal, not with their backs turned.

To bend it left, the player kicks the ball on its right half.

Finally, one of the most efficient and common kicks to execute is the redirect kick. This shot uses the ball's existing kinetic energy to redirect a pass toward goal. Some of the best goals scored off of crosses are simple redirected shots that resemble perfect one-touches. Although they look simple, these shots require good timing and techniques to connect. First, players must use good acceleration to position themselves at the right place to make the play. Second, the proper way to make good contact with the ball is with the inside of the foot, thus presenting a larger contact area. Third, this kick requires eye/foot/ball coordination to make the final connection and redirect the ball in the desired direction.

To bend it right, the player kicks the ball on its left half.

There is no need to "swing" at a fast moving ball to redirect it, as this usually results in a "whiff" or miskick. Instead, players may push the ball in the desired direction using the inside of the foot as in a pass. This can be effective since the ball already has sufficient stored energy to travel. Also, if the ball is crossed from the left, the right foot is the better one to meet it, and vice versa. Trying to kick a ball from originating from the left side with the left foot requires much more timing and accuracy than with the right foot.

Players can exercise the various types of kicks during every practice session. These include stationary kicks, as well as fluid ones on the run or after a pass. Coaches can help improve their players by observing and analyzing their technique. As players understand the differences between these kicks, they'll apply and perform them better.

Advanced Soccer Skills

Chapter V

Coaching and Fitness

- *Fitness for Soccer*

- *Coaching Advice*

- *Soccer for Everyone (kids, men and women)*

- *Select Practice Drills*

Fitness for Soccer

*B*arring serious injury, soccer is an excellent sport for building muscular and cardiovascular strength. Likewise, the rigors of soccer require players to be in relatively good shape to participate in competitive matches, and to avoid injury and exhaustion.

Individuals who started playing at an early age (and stayed in shape throughout their lives) may be the best conditioned athletes to play the game, and therefore they may require less game conditioning than those who started playing later in life. Yet, even highly conditioned soccer players can benefit from cross training and strength regimes.

There are several schools of thought when it comes to soccer fitness, each with its own training and conditioning procedures. As an example, players at the highest levels of German and Italian soccer go through different workouts and training routines. German teams emphasize physical strength and conditioning, so they employ physically demanding training sessions with a large dose of running, sprinting and strength exercises. Italian teams in general have less physical training than their German counterparts, but a higher emphasis on tactical and technical preparation. Both schools undoubtedly work very well since the Italian and German leagues are considered as two of the best in the world, so are the national teams of both nations.

So how does a team that trains physically hard learn tactical awareness and better techniques? Likewise, how do players that emphasize tactics and strategy stay physically fit and strong for match play? The answer is a balanced environment in which to learn the game and stay in shape

Some of the stretching exercises that players can do individually or in groups.

to be able to play it. Coaches who emphasize conditioning do so to give their teams an advantage knowing that their players already understand (or will learn) strategy and tactics. Coaches who emphasize tactical awareness usually believe that players can stay in shape by playing and scrimmaging, and therefore it is best to spend more time on some mind conditioning as well. The debate on which approach is more effective has raged on for a long time without a winner or loser.

Using our examples above, Germany and Italy have each won three world cups, and both nations have been supremely successful at any level in winning championships and producing world-class players. During France '98, however the German team was criticized for its unimaginative fast-paced game, and the Italians for their highly tactical defensive strategy. Both teams lacked the luster of other squads and they unexpectedly exited the tournament before the semifinals. One can argue that this "failure" was not due to the German or Italian soccer philosophy and training techniques, but more because of the available personnel and competition on the field. France won with a team that combines fitness with tactical training, as well as close cooperation and camaraderie between the players.

We mention camaraderie because it is good for team morale, and for motivating players to play and cooperate with each other. Practice without the ball can be hard work, but if the team does it together, it can be fun and challenging. Whatever coaching regime they employ, coaches should consider adding fun and games to their practice sessions.

Soccer players practice to improve their stamina, strength and speed. These requirements differ from one player to the next and sometimes from team to team. Individual needs may vary based on the player's physical shape, age and position. Team requirements vary based on the league level and other factors, such as school limitations or guidelines. Coaches must remember that not everyone must train like professionals do. Pro athletes are paid to compete and do nothing else. They have excellent insurance policies and doctors to protect them. Young and amateur athletes do not have the same protection and cannot maintain the same regimes as professionals.

Coaches and players can adapt some of these exercises to stay in shape and improve their strength and stamina.

- *Light running for warm-up*. Players can jog a couple of laps around the field to warm up before stretching. This light warm-up helps subsequent stretching exercises without undue muscular stress.
- *Stretching exercises*. These can include knee bends, toe touches, and lunges. These collective stretches loosen up the quadriceps, hamstrings and other leg muscles. Another less-used but useful warm-up is the heel stretch. Players can get a good stretch by facing a wall or a pole and leaning and on it and holding the stretch for 20-30 seconds. They can increase the lean slightly for a bigger stretch.
- *Kicking warm-up*. Players can pair up or have small passing circles to kick the ball around which helps loosen their legs and feet.
- *Organized drills*. After players warm up, coaches can put them through the day's drills for 30-60 minutes depending on the time available. It's best to vary the drilling pace from active to slow and so on. Running crosses can be followed by stationary kicking, which in turn can be followed by another running exercise and a stationary one. This gives players time to rest and pace themselves,

as well as keeping them active enough to keep them warmed up and involved. Coaches can rotate and vary the exercises from day to day, or they can customize them to meet team and individual player needs.

- *No contact scrimmage.* We emphasize NO CONTACT in a scrimmage so players consciously try to keep the practice injury free. Injury during practice can defeat the purpose and reverse individual and team progress. Coaches can use a scrimmage to watch teamwork and help players with tactical and technical issues. Many coaches either participate in scrimmages or walk on the field to teach players as play continues. Scrimmages can go from 30 to 90 minutes to provide players realistic game conditioning.
- *Hollow sprints.* Since soccer requires frequent sprints and running, players can line up for field-length sprints followed by easy jogs for the same distance. Since these are anaerobic sprints, players can rest again before repeating the exercise several times depending on their physical shape and endurance. This is perhaps the best and most aerobic/anaerobic exercise for a soccer player since it increases stamina, strength and in some instances speed. The adage "you can't coach speed" isn't necessarily accurate since many players never truly practice sprints and therefore do not discover their full potential.
- *Weight lifting and other cross training.* Leg presses and leg extensions build strong muscles to add strength and durability. Players should also add some hamstring-building exercises to develop these sensitive muscles.

Since it may not be possible to accomplish all these exercises in one day or session, players can customize their schedule to fit as many exercises as possible in a week. Customization also means concentrating on some aspects that need development and decreasing others that don't need as much. If players do all of the above and perhaps add more customized exercises (e.g., cycling, running), they should be able to increase their stamina and strength for soccer, as well as reduce their risk of injury.

A jog around the field is an excellent way to warm up before stretching.

Interestingly, the above recipe is a mixture of exercise with and without the ball, and it shouldn't hinder tactical and technical learning which can take place during drills, scrimmages, and classroom sessions. Scrimmages have the advantage of improving skill *and* conditioning, and most players enjoy scrimmaging and playing more than they enjoy structured drills. In order to obtain maximum soccer fitness, however, coaches should use running and conditioning exercises to supplement game induced conditioning. It is also important for coaches and players to have time off to rest the body. Many advocate resting every other day, or exercising different muscle groups in an alternating schedule.

This can vary depending on the players' age and conditioning, but alternating workout days is a safe and effective procedure in most cases.

Other stretching exercises that players can do individually or in groups.

Juggling is an excellent way to warm up and improve skill.

Coaching Advice

*T*here are thousands of volunteer and paid soccer coaches throughout the U.S. and every country in the world. Soccer coaches in the U.S. are probably less recognized and appreciated than those in other sports, and therefore many leave soccer in pursuit of other opportunities. Consequently, many amateur and even high school coaches are "fill-ins" with little knowledge or passion for the game.

Many coaches with or without accreditation, however, are excellent teachers of the game. Many have played soccer since they were quite young and they know how to teach the technical and tactical aspects of soccer. The lucky ones who get paid for coaching may have better conditions not because of their modest salaries, but rather because of the athletes they coach. Paid coaches usually work with players who are willing to follow directions and learn the game, unlike players who pay to play on weekends, and therefore may not always follow coaching, even if it were good, free advice.

Our best advice to soccer coaches and players is to *simplify* the game and not complicate it. One of the greatest mistakes many coaches make is treating soccer like mainstream American sports such as football and baseball. These coaches frequently conduct highly structured practices and scrimmages that complicate rather than simplify the game.

This isn't to say that coaches shouldn't conduct practices related to a certain area or position. Ideally, the coach should explain why he's running this kind of practice, or giving the activity a "value." For example, practicing outside defense to make sure the outside backs and their support players understand their duties and improve their skills. The coach may introduce some restrictions or cones to the exercise, but it may be best to keep it as simple as possible, such as having some players attack, while others defend on the outside. Restrictions may mean staying within a certain area, having uneven numbers against each other, or being unable to play both ways.

Scrimmages are a perfect time for coaching. Many coaches walk between their players during scrimmages to give advice and make observations.

Cones are also used in practice, sometimes way too much! It's not highly unusual to see confused players running around clueless trying to figure out which way to go and with whom. There are many coaches who use cones for nothing more than boundaries and the all-popular dribbling slalom. Too many cones and micro drills can become quite confusing and add confusion and stress to the practice session. It's probably a lot more effective to have a free flowing and fun workout that also covers certain skills.

Too many variables, cones and restrictions can sometimes confuse players during practice rather than develop them efficiently.

The following are some points of advice that can help coaches succeed and last in this delicate profession:

- *Be positive*. There are many well-known basketball and football coaches who use negative tactics (sometimes bordering on abuse) to motivate their players. We disagree with these tactics for any sport, especially for soccer, which normally features intelligent and articulate athletes. Good soccer coaches generally pick out athletes with good work ethics and character that will do their best under any circumstance. Therefore, the coach should set the example by being positive and supportive, especially during adversity. By doing so, he can get the most of his players who respect and appreciate his leadership and compassion. The best coaching adage in this regard states: "Shout praise and whisper criticism." Even when they make mistakes, players do not appreciate being criticized publicly. They do, however, appreciate public praise!

- *Keep things in perspective.* As we were finishing this book, the German national team lost a game to Brazil in the '99 Confederation Cup by a score of 4-0. This is significant in that even a three-time World Champion can lose games to a better team by a wide margin. No coach wants to see his team lose a game, especially by several goals. The fact is, however, that there will always be a better team that can and should beat his team. Obviously, this coach should try to win or tie the game, but if he loses, he should accept the facts and make something positive come out of the experience.

- *Stay organized.* Regardless of what system he employs, the coach should try to stay organized and have a workable system for practice and games. By doing so, he can keep the players' attention and discipline.

- *Be professional.* A coach who looks and acts professionally can ask his players to do the same. This means dressing appropriately for practice and games, as well as acting professionally in public, such as at hotels and restaurants (this applies to recreational and non-recreational teams). Referees in general will also respect coaches who act professionally over those who don't.

- *Be compassionate.* Compassion and coaching go hand in hand. A good coach appreciates everything his players do for the team, and will back his players up in times of need. This could mean helping them with personal and professional problems off the field, as well as on the field. Even if a coach is unable to help out, a compassionate one will at least lend an ear and try to give moral and emotional support. This personal compassion usually pays off many times when it comes to performance and loyalty.

- *Mix talk and action.* A coach should not refrain from talking to his team and only concentrating on drills. After all, coaching is about giving direction and teaching the game, and a lot of this can be done just before or during practice. A coach should keep in mind the temperature and try to economize on words when it's cold, and talk more when it's hot thus ensuring his players don't freeze up or overheat.

- *Study the game for God's sake!* Even the most honorable and compassionate coaches need to thoroughly understand the game and its intricacies. One area that most new coaches can improve upon is the history of the game. Having grown up in a baseball environment, some employed soccer coaches today know baseball's history better than the history of soccer. By learning the history and evolution of soccer, a coach can have a point of reference as to what style or philosophy to employ. Additional study includes attending coaching schools and learning to coach the technical and tactical aspects of the game.

- *Make it fun.* Is it a coincidence that Brazil is the world's best soccer country? We don't think so! Brazilians play soccer in the street, during work and school breaks, at picnics, and whenever they can. This passion stems from the immense fun that these players get from playing "the beautiful game." The result of this passion and fun is a country that can field two or three *reserve* national teams that can beat the starting teams of most other nations. Although coaching Brazilians is quite different culturally and technically than coaching North Americans or other players, by making soccer a fun experience, coaches can expect players to return for more, and to improve at a reasonable pace.

There are many roads to success, and coaches can have their own style, as well as set their own pace and philosophy. Success, in fact, is measured in different ways by coaches, organizations, and players. Whether wins, fun, attendance, safety, or other standards measure it, success should always be measured with progress. If a team sets realistic goals for itself and it meets them, then this can be termed a success. The coach is the person most responsible for meeting and measuring these goals, and for keeping the team focused and united behind its objectives.

One-on-one instruction is an essential aspect of coaching.

Soccer for Everyone (men, women and children)

This book was largely inspired by the need for people in the U.S. not only to understand the game of soccer, but the universal soccer culture as a whole. Soccer is indeed a sport for the masses and a game for *everyone* who wants to play or watch. Kids in the slums of Brazil, men in the streets of Mexico and women playing in California share a great love and understanding for the game. American players are unique in that they espouse and play soccer over other mainstream sports, such as football and baseball. What happens to the crop of great players after graduating from high school is a totally different story. Most fade away into various other mainstream activities, and a select few keep an interest in soccer.

Having established and managed a very popular soccer web site, this author quickly recognized that soccer in the U.S. needs a "culture" as it exists in any other country. Our Soccer-HQ web site regularly receives inquiries ranging from the simplest to the most basic. This suggests that many people don't know soccer very well and are looking for information that they cannot find readily. It is up to soccer players, coaches, clubs, schools, and indeed web sites to educate the masses and promote the game in any way possible.

Perhaps the greatest number of inquiries received on Soccer-HQ's web site dealt with questions on coaching very young children (5-10 years old). After answering the first few of these inquiries, our staff decided to have one patented answer for all: Don't worry about "coaching" young children, just ensure that they play and HAVE FUN. It's too early to coach these young kids beyond the basics (shooting, passing, trapping), and unless they grow to love the game, they won't stick around for further coaching. In fact, it seems that too much direction and coaching can cause confusion and undue stress (for both coach and players). It's okay to have a parent/coach to ensure the kids show up on time and play on the right field, etc. But essentially, simplify the game for the children, and do not over-coach.

Many parents and coaches should coach less and let the little ones play and have fun.

Young teenagers are the perfect candidates for learning as part of their lifestyle and development. At 12 or 13, these players can master a wider array of skills, as well as understand drills and basic tactical concepts. This is a perfect time to start training players in certain positions based on their skill and physiques. For example, quick and short players with good shooting skills make good candidates for attackers, while larger, sturdier players may make better center backs. Although aptitude and compatibility contribute to decision making, it's important not to stereotype children and not force them to play positions they do not enjoy.

As they reach high school level, players become naturally competitive and serious about the game. This is when good coaching can help them improve and win. Coaches at this point should work on correcting and improving style, as well as teaching tactics, strategy and winning. High school players can also learn valuable intangibles, such as teamwork, good work ethic and determination. High school level soccer is perhaps the most critical phase of player and team development in America. The fact that there is a small percentage of quality high school coaches and programs may explain why soccer has taken a back seat to football and baseball in this country. One way to avoid this obstacle is for parents to send their children to soccer camps, as well as helping them learn independently of their high school program. This of course does not apply if the particular high school program is a good one in the parents' opinion.

College programs have the luxury of choosing their players and coaching the right mix of talent. There are some very quality programs in the U.S. today for both men and women. North Carolina, Notre Dame and Florida have excellent women's programs, while Virginia, UCLA and Indiana are excellent examples of men's soccer. Between them, these universities have produced the greatest number of soccer players for professional leagues and the women and men's national teams. There's no doubt that the head coaches and staff of these colleges have elevated the game to a science, and as other institutions catch up to them, the quality of soccer in this country will surely improve. We listed the above examples as some of the best, but fortunately, there are many more excellent programs around the nation that one can find in college soccer listings.

The progression after college is a narrow one for the few gifted athletes who go on to play professionally here and abroad. Perhaps the fact that only a few American players play abroad is a judgment against the quantity of players produced in this country. One of the most gifted college athletes of our era, Claudio Reyna, plays professionally in Europe (Germany, and now Scotland). A final product of Virginia, Reyna quickly established himself as a world-class talent, and hopefully, there will be many more soccer athletes like him. We also hope MLS (Major League Soccer) will continue to grow and crowds will keep attending professional soccer games around the nation.

For the grand majority of players who don't play professionally, there are various semi-professional and recreational leagues to fill their needs and keep them playing. There are probably more registered soccer players in this nation than any European country, which attests to the popularity of soccer as a recreational sport in the U.S. *Soccer America* magazine is an excellent resource to find local leagues and clubs around the nation. It is this recreational label on soccer that makes it such a popular sport for kids and young adults. Parents view soccer as an excellent athletic activity for their kids, so do millions of adults who participate in league and pick-up games.

Since we believe soccer is a game for everyone, the knowledge of this book applies to men, women, boys or girls. American women have shown that they can play the game as well as men, and they have two

World Cup titles to prove it. Regardless of social and personal criteria, however, nature meant women and men to be different, so coaches and players ought to take these differences into consideration.

Let's start with some of the physical differences. Although male athletes are generally faster and stronger than female athletes, women have shown that they can master the technical and tactical aspects of the game just as well as men can. Anyone who watched the top teams in the most recent Women's World Cup in the U.S. can attest to these facts. The Chinese and U.S. teams in particular included players with excellent skills, athleticism and tactical savvy only found at the highest levels of the game.

It does not matter whether women are coached by male or female coaches as long as they respond well to the coach.

Some of the physical aspects that differentiate between men and women (other than speed and strength) have to do with female health issues such as menstruation and bone structure. The latest research into women athletes indicates that women that menstruate less than 7 times a year should see a doctor since they may be good candidates for early osteoporosis. Even the strongest and healthiest looking athletes may have the bones of much older women if they do not diagnose and treat this condition early. Coaches should discuss this condition with their female athletes. Male coaches who are not comfortable with discussing the subject should ask a female assistant or trainer to do so since this is such an important health issue.

Other aspects that separate men and women are psychological. Although these factors vary from person to person and culture to culture, it is generally believed that female athletes are a lot more receptive to positive reinforcement than to challenges and confrontation. Even the most hardened female athletes are still women that represent their upbringing, which is usually quite different than that of men in the same society. Women are generally much less comfortable with pressure, lack of civility, and many forms of macho competitiveness, whether exhibited by their male coach or any other person.

So should male coaches stay away from coaching women? The answer to this is obviously "no!" Some of the most successful coaches of women's soccer are men, such as Anson Dorrance of North Carolina fame, and Tony DiCicco of the U.S. national team. Obviously these gentlemen have done extremely well coaching women, and have found the right combination of compassion and discipline to produce some of the world's best female players and teams. Women have also done quite well in coaching other women, and some may have an advantage of knowing their sex much better than most men do. In the end, it doesn't really matter whether the coach is a man or a woman as long as the coach and players share mutual goals and respect for each other.

Select Practice Drills

Coaches and teams need to have some practice drills to help them improve technically and tactically. There is literally hundreds of existing and newly devised drills that can help teams prepare and improve. The best advice for new teams and coaches is to simplify! Some of the drills devised by new and inexperienced coaches are so complicated that even the most experienced players find them hard to follow. This over-dependence on drilling can sometimes confuse and bore players rather than teach them.

Therefore, we suggest simplifying any form of exercise or drill to the point of making it natural and fun. The idea of drills is repetition to improve skill and fitness. Therefore, coaches can devise any simple skills that improve techniques and tactics. This customization of drills is an ideal way to run a practice before and after a scrimmage.

The following pages contain pictures of some skill-improving drills that players can do on their own, as well in small or large numbers. These drills rely more on repetition and technique than on confusing cones and drilling rules. Leave the rules for the actual game!

Players can improve their skill by juggling on their own. No need for a coach or teammates!

This simple warm-up drill teaches passing and trapping. The players line up opposite each other; one ball per two players. They pass to each other and trap the ball back and forth.

The cone slalom is probably one of the most popular drills in soccer. It teaches control, cutting and acceleration. Coaches can make this drill into a fun game by timing their players or rewarding improvement.

Two players can line up opposite each other and shoot a dead ball at each other. They can gradually vary the distance as they warm up. This exercise teaches accurate kicking and receiving.

This variation on the previous exercise teaches players to volley the ball. Each player can toss the ball to himself and volley or half-volley it to his waiting teammate.

In this shooting drill, players line up with one ball each. They dribble at a cone (defender), simulate beating the defender and take a quick shot on goal as fast as they can. The exercise teaches players the importance of releasing the ball early when covered, as well as improving the sub-skills associated with dribbling and shooting.

This is a simple exercise that teaches players to head the ball while warming up. Note the constantly shifting legs and bodies to ensure heading the ball properly.

Another heading exercise involves having the players line up, while a coach or a teammate tosses the ball in the air for them to attack and head on goal.

One-on-one training is very important for teaching players how to play their positions. Here the defender learns how to cover and contain an attacker.

... or the attacker (left) learns how to draw a defender and go by her.

In this drill, players dribble the ball about 15 yards, turn and dribble back to a waiting teammate who repeats the drill with the same ball. This exercise emphasizes turning with the ball and giving possession to a teammate heading in the opposite direction.

Players should practice taking penalties whenever possible. A goalie is not necessary, but having one in goal adds pressure and gives him some goalkeeping practice as well.

In this drill, players line up in two opposing lines. A player dribbles a ball to the other line where another from that line takes possession of the ball while the first player peels off. The objective is to train players to communicate and change possession/direction smoothly.

An important game-related tactic that teams can practice is forming and maintaining an offside line.

As part of any practice or scrimmage, coaches should ensure their players take regular thow-ins to improve technique and tactics.

*One of the most useful crossing exercises involves forming two lines of
players. Players from the first line dribble the ball down the wing and cross
it to players from the second line who head it on goal. Note how the player
in white waits onside for the ball to be crossed.*

This goalkeeping exercise has the goalie hustling to block shots coming from various angles as indicated by the cones. Players can take shots at the goalie for more realism. This tiring exercise teaches the goalkeeper the mechanics of shifting angles, as well as giving him an excellent workout.

Epilogue

The New Soccer Attitudes

*O*n any Sunday in Southern California, one can drive by any park in a Hispanic area and find soccer activity. Hispanics in the U.S. have always embraced soccer as a primary sport that they play and support throughout their lives. Whether they play in organized leagues or in run down parks with little equipment and organization, these educated soccer fans exhibit a true passion and understanding for the game.

Mainstream America still has a lot to catch up to the rest of the world in this international sport. The fact that the U.S. finished last in the '98 World Cup in France did not help the sport grow here, but the U.S. women made up with an excellent World Cup in '99 and a well-deserved first place finish. Our web site response showed that the public in general follows media coverage and showed great interest in soccer during the Women's World Cup. Unfortunately, this interest subsided soon after the event ended.

The recent women's World Cup introduced a new crop of young players to soccer. Hopefully, school and community programs will do enough to keep the majority of these players involved for a long time. Otherwise, we will need a World Cup event in the U.S. every few years, which is not a realistic wish.

This is perhaps why we think the rest of the nation should embrace soccer and MLS as much as the Hispanic community has done for a long time. An educated soccer nation will produce much better players, teams and leagues.

To learn more about soccer, log on to our web site: WWW.Soccer-HQ.com

The future of American soccer is here already!

Index

A

AC Milan 42, 50
Age 130
American Players 19
Argentina 52, 68, 103
Armas, Chris 77

B

Back pass 114
Baggio, Roberto 69, 103
Baresi, Franco 50
Batistuta, Gabriel 68
Belgium 52
Brazil 50, 60, 77, 103, 141, 144
Breitner, Paul 42

C

Camaraderie 132
Campos, Jorge 32
Cardiovascular 130
Carlos, Roberto 100
Central defense 43
Central midfielders 58, 60
Coaching 129
College programs 146
    Florida 146
    Indiana 146
    North Carolina 146
    Notre Dame 146
    UCLA 146

Preparation
    Tactical 130
    Technical 130

R

Real Madrid 42, 100
Return pass 115
Reyna, Claudio 77, 147
Romania 98
Ronaldo 68
Running 130

S

Schmeichel, Peter 32
Scotland 147
Scrimmage 134
Skill 73
Soccer America 147
Soccer-HQ 144
Space 121
    Occupied 121
    Unoccupied 121
Spain 100
Sprinting 130
Sprints 134
Stopper 48
Strategy 71
Strength 130
Stretching 133
Sweeper 48, 50

T

Tackling 16
    Block Tackle 16